MORE POWER

SUPERSIZING THE WORKING OF THE HOLY SPIRIT FOR LIFE AND MINISTRY

BILL JUONI

A Practical Handbook on the Baptism in the
Holy Spirit and Living a Spirit-filled Life

ISBN: 978-0692778937

First printing 2016

Printed in the United States of America

DEDICATION

This book is dedicated to my wife, Beth. You have been my faithful partner in the many facets of ministry that our journey of serving the Lord together has brought us. First serving the Lord as laymen in the local church while I worked in retail management. Then serving the Lord for twenty years as Lead Pastors after the Lord called us into the ministry. And now traveling across the country and overseas together in ministry since 1998. What an exciting journey it has been serving the Lord together.

TABLE OF CONTENTS

ACKNOWLEDGMENTS

I would like to acknowledge and thank the many people who helped make this book possible.

I would like to thank my wife, Beth, who not only has been a faithful co-laborer in ministry but also helped make this book possible through her computer knowledge, technical advice and proofreading the manuscript.

I also would like to thank the many pastors across the country and missionaries overseas who have encouraged me to write a book and put into writing what I presented in their places of ministry. Their encouraging words of "you should put this in a book," and "you need to write a book" encouraged me to write this book.

INTRODUCTION

One of the things we see wherever we minister are the golden arches of McDonalds. We have found them across America and in most of the countries of the world where we have ministered.

McDonalds had a very popular deal a while back where you could "supersize" your order. You could get a much larger size or portion for just a little bit more money. It was still the same food item, just a whole lot more of it.

This book deals with "supersizing" the working of the Holy Spirit in the life of a believer—a greater working of the same Holy Spirit that already dwells in the life of the believer.

Another illustration I heard was from a pastor who pictured the Holy Spirit, who dwells in every believer, as being like the pilot light in a gas oven, a gas water heater or a gas furnace. All these appliances have the flame of the pilot light in them but when you turn on the oven or increase the temperature of the water heater or furnace; the pilot light bursts into a large flame. It's still fire, just a whole lot more of it. The flame has been "supersized."

After a person gives his life to Christ and experiences the working of the Holy Spirit in his life, it's normal and natural to ask; how can I have more? How can I have more power for everyday living? How can I have more power to deal with the issues of everyday life and the issues of the world I live in? How can I have more power to live the Christian life? How can I have more power to be what Jesus wants me to be and to do what Jesus wants me to do?

In the following chapters, we will show you how to experience more power for everyday living and for ministry. Every believer can "supersize" the working of the Holy Spirit in his life.

Chapter One

EVERY BELIEVER AND THE HOLY SPIRIT

On his Byline radio program, host Pastor Dan Betzer told about a man who called his travel agent to make a reservation. He said, "I want to go from Chicago to Hippopotamus, New York." The agent was a bit shaken and said, "Are you sure that's the name of the town? I've looked up every airport in the country and can't find a Hippopotamus anywhere." The man said, "Don't be silly. Everyone knows where it is. Look at your map!" The agent scoured the map of New York again and finally offered, "You don't mean Buffalo, do you?" The man responded, "Yeah! That's it! I knew it was a big animal."[1]

That man was very sincere, but being sincere didn't mean he was right. Sometimes the Holy Spirit can be a topic of confusion and misunderstanding in which people can be very sincere in what they believe, but that doesn't mean they are right.

Regardless of the church background someone comes from, that church most likely believes in and acknowledges the reality of the Holy Spirit—the third person of the Trinity. Liturgical churches; such as Catholic, Lutheran, Methodist, Episcopal, etc., believe in the Holy Spirit. Evangelical churches; such as Baptist, Nazarene, Evangelical Free, etc., believe in the Holy Spirit. Pentecostal churches; such as the Assemblies of God, Church of God, Four Square, etc., believe in the Holy Spirit.

The Bible teaches us about the Trinity; the Father, the Son, and the Holy Spirit. The Bible tells us that today the Father is seated in heaven, the Son (Jesus) is seated at His right hand, and the Holy Spirit dwells on earth and within believers.

While Jesus was ministering on earth, He said it would be necessary for Him to leave so the Holy Spirit could come.

"Nevertheless I tell you the truth. It is to your advantage that I go away; or if I do not go away, the Helper (Holy Spirit) will not come to you; but if I depart, I will send Him to you" (John 16:7 NKJV).

EVERY BELIEVER WAS DRAWN BY THE HOLY SPIRIT

Every person who has ever become a believer, a follower of Jesus, was drawn by the Holy Spirit. The Father draws pre-believers to His Son, Jesus, through the Holy Spirit. Jesus said,

"No one can come to me unless the Father who sent me draws him..." (John 6:44 NKJV).

12

So, how does the Father draw people to Jesus? Through the Holy Spirit. The Holy Spirit draws pre-believers to Jesus in three ways:

1. The Holy Spirit shows people their sin. He opens their spiritual eyes to the sin in their life. He convicts them of their sin. Jesus said,

   "And when He (the Holy Spirit) has come, He will convict the world of sin, and of righteousness and of judgment" (John 16:8 NKJV).

2. The Holy Spirit shows people the love of Christ and the love of God. He shows them how much they are loved. Paul wrote,

   "Or do you despise the riches of His goodness, forbearance, and longsuffering, not knowing that the goodness of God leads you to repentance" (Romans 2:4 NKJV).

   In the film *The Cross and the Switchblade*, a movie depicting David Wilkerson's ministry to the gangs in New York City, there is a scene where David Wilkerson is being threatened by a gang member with a knife. David Wilkerson says to the gang member with the knife, "you can cut me to pieces, but every piece is going to cry out how much Jesus loves you." That gang member didn't hurt Wilkerson and later said he couldn't forget those words. Through those words, the Holy Spirit was letting him know how much Jesus loved him.

3. The Holy Spirit shows people their need to accept Christ. Jesus said,

"Behold I stand at the door and knock. If anyone hears My voice and opens the door, I will come in..." (Revelation 3:20 NKJV).

While the actual context deals with Jesus knocking on the door of the church at Laodicea, it can also picture how Jesus knocks on the door of the heart of the pre-believer; asking to be let in. How can Jesus knock on the door of the heart of the pre-believer when He is in heaven? Through the Holy Spirit.

The Holy Spirit draws people to the truth. The Holy Spirit convicts them of their sin. The Holy Spirit reveals Jesus is the answer to their helplessness and hopelessness. Without Jesus they are separated from God. The Holy Spirit says to a person; you need Jesus, come to Jesus and Jesus wants you to come to Him.

In *The Whisper Test*, Mary Ann Bird writes:

I grew up knowing I was different, and I hated it. I was born with a cleft palate, and when I started school, my classmates made it clear to me how I looked to others: a little girl with a misshapen lip, crooked nose, lopsided teeth and garbled speech. When schoolmates asked, "What happened to your lip?" I'd tell them I'd fallen and cut it on a piece of glass. Somehow it seemed more acceptable to have suffered an accident than to have been born different. I was convinced that no one outside my family could love me. There was, however, a teacher in the second grade whom we all adored, Mrs. Leonard by name. She was a short, round, happy, sparkling lady. Annually we had a hearing test.

Mrs. Leonard gave the test to everyone in the class and finally it was my turn. I knew from past years that as we stood against the door and covered one ear, the teacher sitting at her desk would whisper something, and we would have to repeat it back–things like "The sky is blue" or "Do you have new shoes?" I waited there for those words that God must have put into her mouth, those seven words that changed my life. Mrs. Leonard said, in her whisper, "I wish you were my little girl."[2]

God says to every person deformed by sin, "I wish you were my son" or "I wish you were my daughter."

That's what God says through the Holy Spirit to every person who has been deformed by sin. Which includes all of us because we all have sinned. God says, "I wish you were my son" or "I wish you were my daughter." The Father draws people to Jesus through the Holy Spirit.

That's why we pray for our pre-believing friends, neighbors and family members. That God through the Holy Spirit will draw them to Jesus. That God through the Holy Spirit will penetrate their heart, convict them of their sin and open their eyes spiritually to see their need of Jesus. The choice to respond will always be theirs, and God will never take away that freedom of choice but God has amazing ways to work in people's lives to bring them to Jesus.

The encouragement is, don't quit praying for your pre-believing friends, neighbors and family members. As you pray for them, the Holy Spirit is loosed to work on their hearts. No one is beyond being reached for Jesus.

Every believer was drawn by the Holy Spirit.

EVERY BELIEVER HAS RECEIVED
THE HOLY SPIRIT

Not only has every believer been drawn to Jesus by the Holy Spirit but every believer has received the Holy Spirit. Every believer has the Holy Spirit dwelling within them.

We find this illustrated from the lives of Jesus' original disciples. John 7:37-39 tells us:

"On the last and greatest day of the feast, Jesus stood and cried out saying, 'If anyone thirsts, let Him come to Me and drink. He who believes in Me, as the scripture has said, out of his heart will flow rivers of living water.' But this He spoke concerning the Spirit, whom those believing in Him would receive; for the Holy Spirit was not yet given, because Jesus was not yet glorified" (NKJV).

Jesus said this regarding the Holy Spirit to his disciples, but the Holy Spirit was not yet given because Jesus had not yet been glorified.

This meant the Spirit had not yet been given because Jesus had not yet been crucified and resurrected. Prior to His crucifixion Jesus said in John 12:23-24,

"The hour has come that the Son of Man should be glorified. Most assuredly, I say to you, unless a grain of wheat falls into the ground and dies, it remains alone; but if it dies, it produces much grain" (NKJV).

Regarding this portion of scripture the notes in the Life in the Spirit Study Bible say, "This refers to Jesus' glory resulting from His death and resurrection..."[3]

Jesus then carried out his earthly ministry and was crucified on a cross in payment for our sins. He died and was buried, but three days later He rose from the dead with a glorified, resurrected body. Then Jesus appeared to His disciples, after His resurrection, with His glorified body, and in John 20:22 it says,

"And when He had said this, He breathed on them, and said to them, 'Receive the Holy Spirit'" (NKJV).

Jesus breathed upon His disciples and said, "Receive the Holy Spirit." Now they had the Holy Spirit dwelling in them in the same way every believer has the Holy Spirit dwelling within them.

Paul writing to the believers in Rome said,

"...the Spirit of God dwells in you..." (Romans 8:9 NKJV).

"...the Spirit of Him who raised Jesus from the dead dwells in you..." (Romans 8:11 NKJV).

The moment a person makes a life commitment to Christ, the Holy Spirit comes and dwells within. The Bible refers to this as being "born of the Spirit."

"...that which is born of the Spirit..." (John 3:6 NKJV).

Every follower of Christ has the Holy Spirit dwelling within them. The Holy Spirit, who came;

1) as promised by Jesus

"And I will pray to the Father, and He will give you another Helper, that He may abide with you forever–the Spirit..." (John 14:16-17 NKJV).

2) as an equal part of the Trinity

"...in the name of the Father and of the Son and of the Holy Spirit..." (Matthew 28:19-20 NKJV).

3) as a helper

"But the Helper, the Holy Spirit, whom the Father will send..." (John 14:26 NKJV).

The Holy Spirit helps followers of Christ in several ways:

1. the Holy Spirit teaches us

"...not in words which man's wisdom teaches but which the Holy Spirit teaches..." (I Corinthians 2:13 NKJV).

2. the Holy Spirit comforts us

"But the Comforter, which is the Holy Ghost, whom the Father will send..." (John 14:26 KJV).

3. the Holy Spirit gives us the words to say

"For the Holy Spirit will teach you in that very hour what you ought to say" (Luke 12:12 NKJV).

4. the Holy Spirit gives us direction

As they ministered to the Lord and fasted, the Holy Spirit said, "Now separate to Me

Barnabas and Saul for the work to which I have called them." (Acts 13:2 NKJV).

5. the Holy Spirit gives life

"It is the Spirit who gives life; the flesh profits nothing. The words that I speak to you are spirit, and they are life." (John 6:63 NKJV).

6. the Holy Spirit guides us to truth

"...the Spirit of truth has come, He will guide you into all truth..." (John 16:13 NKJV).

7. the Holy Spirit brings things Christ has said to our remembrance

"...He will teach you all things, and bring to your remembrance all things I said to you." (John 14:26 NKJV).

8. the Holy Spirit convicts us of sin

"...when He (the Holy Spirit) has come, He will convict the world of sin..." (John 16:8 NKJV).

9. the Holy Spirit testifies of Christ to us

"But when the helper comes, whom I shall send to you from the Father, the Spirit of truth who proceeds from the Father, He will testify of Me" (John 15:26 NKJV).

10. the Holy Spirit bears the fruit of the Spirit in us

"But the fruit of the Spirit is love, joy, peace, longsuffering, kindness, goodness, faithfulness, gentleness, self-control..." (Galatians 5:22-23 NKJV)

The Holy Spirit dwells in every believer and is endeavoring to do all these things in the life of the believer. Since this is the case, shouldn't we desire as much of the working of the Holy Spirit in our lives as possible?

EVERY BELIEVER CAN RECEIVE THE BAPTISM IN THE HOLY SPIRIT

Thus far we have looked at how every believer was drawn to Christ by the Holy Spirit and how every believer has the Holy Spirit dwelling within him, but there is one more area, the baptism in the Holy Spirit. The baptism in the Holy Spirit can revolutionize a Christian's life, increasing what the Holy Spirit is already doing in his life.

As we mentioned in the introduction, the baptism in the Holy Spirit is like "supersizing" an order at McDonald's. Or like a pilot light bursting into flame when you turn on the gas oven or increase the temperature of a gas furnace or gas water heater.

This was the experience Jesus emphasized just prior to His ascension to heaven. In fact, Jesus' last words before ascending to heaven were about the baptism in the Holy Spirit. When people get down to their last words and time is short, they talk about what's important, don't they? Listen to what Jesus thought was so important that He talked about this with His last words.

"for John truly baptized with water, but you shall be baptized with the Holy Spirit not many days from now... you shall receive power when the Holy Spirit has come upon you; and you shall be witnesses to Me in Jerusalem, and in all Judea and

Samaria, and to the end of the earth." (Acts 1:5 and 8 NKJV).

Jesus told His disciples, who already had the Holy Spirit dwelling in them in the same way every believer does, "don't leave Jerusalem without this." Don't start your ministry without this.

Jesus said,

"Behold, I send the promise of My Father upon you; but tarry in the city of Jerusalem until you are endued with power from on high." (Luke 24:49 NKJV).

This experience was

- after salvation
- separate from salvation
- for those who already had the Holy Spirit dwelling in them in the same way every believer does
- important in the eyes of Jesus

This promise was made to believers who already had the Holy Spirit dwelling within them.

Misconceptions can cause a believer to miss out on this wonderful promise.

Time magazine carried the following news item illustrating how misconceptions and suspicions can cause someone to miss out on a great gift.

"When the Post Office in Troy, Michigan, summoned Michael Achorn to pick up a 2-foot-long, 40-pound package, his wife Margaret, cheerfully went to accept it. But as she drove back to her office in Detroit, she began to worry. The box was from Montgomery Ward, but the sender, Edward Achorn, was unknown to Margaret and her husband, despite the identical last name. What if the thing was a bomb? She telephoned postal authorities... The bomb squad soon arrived with eight squad cars and an armored truck. They took the suspected bomb in the armored truck to a remote tip of Belle Isle in the middle of the Detroit River. There they wrapped the detonating cord around the package and, as they say in the bomb business, 'opened it remotely.' When the debris settled, all that was left intact was the factory warranty for the contents: a $450 stereo AM-FM receiver and a tape deck console. Now the only mystery is who is Edward Achorn and why did he send Michael and Margaret such a nice Christmas present?[4]

Misconceptions can cause us to miss out on great gifts that are available to us. It can happen regarding the gift of the baptism in the Holy Spirit.

Five Misconceptions People Have Regarding the Baptism in the Holy Spirit

1. *Some have wrongly been told that the baptism in the Holy Spirit is only for some believers.*

The Bible tells us the baptism in the Holy Spirit is for all believers. When Peter was explaining the outpouring of the baptism in the Holy Spirit on the Day of Pentecost in Acts 2, he said,

"For the promise is to you and to your children, and to all who are afar off, as many as the Lord our God will call" (Acts 2:39 NKJV).

Notice the words; *you, your children, to all* and *as many*. The baptism in the Holy Spirit is for all believers, any believer and every believer.

2. *Some have wrongly been told the baptism in the Holy Spirit ended with the book of Acts.*

Notice again in the previous verse that the baptism in the Holy Spirit was also for those "who are afar off" meaning future generations and for "as many as the Lord our God will call." The baptism in the Holy Spirit was not going to end with the book of Acts but would also be for future generations. For as many as would come to Christ in the future.

Another portion of scripture that confirms that the baptism in the Holy Spirit would continue is found in Luke 3:16 where John the Baptist is speaking of Jesus.

"...I baptize you with water. But one more powerful than I will come, the thongs of whose sandals I am not worthy to untie. He will baptize you with the Holy Spirit..." (Luke 3:16 NIV).

The phrase "He will baptize you with the Holy Spirit" uses the present participle meaning "he who will continue to baptize".[5] Therefore the reference is not only to the first outpouring of the Holy Spirit baptism at Pentecost but also for future generations to come.

3. *Some have wrongly been told the baptism in the Holy Spirit is received at salvation.*

The Holy Spirit was received the moment someone became a believer, a Christ follower, but that is not the same as the baptism in the Holy Spirit and being baptized in the Holy Spirit. As was mentioned earlier; the disciples, prior to Pentecost, already had the Holy Spirit dwelling in them in the same way every believer has the Holy Spirit dwelling in them. Being baptized in the Holy Spirit is a separate, additional experience.

That's why Paul asked the believers he came across in Ephesus,

"...Have ye received the Holy Ghost since ye believed? And they said unto him, We have not so much as heard whether there be any Holy Ghost" (Acts 19:2 KJV).

The New King James Version translates it this way,

"...Did you receive the Holy Spirit when you believed?" So they said to him, "We have not so much as heard whether there is a Holy Spirit" (Acts 19:2 NKJV).

According to Strong's Exhaustive Concordance, the word that is translated "since" in the King James Version and "when" in the New King James Version is the Greek word "apo." The word means "away from" or "separate." Paul was asking these believers, have you received the Holy Spirit "away from" or "separate from" when you became believers. He was asking them if they had received this additional experience of being baptized in the Holy Spirit.

According to Dr. George O. Wood, Paul's question would have read like this in the original Greek, "Having believed, did you receive the Holy Spirit?"[6] Meaning, having believed, since then have you received the baptism in the Holy Spirit.

I read in an article where Dr. Stanley Horton commenting further on this portion of scripture said that since these disciples claimed to be believers, the baptism in the Holy Spirit should have been the next step after believing. "When" would refer to how the baptism in the Holy Spirit would have been the normal next step but not meaning at the same moment.[7]

The notes in the Life in the Spirit Study Bible explain this passage in this way–"...Paul's question here refers to the baptism in the Holy Spirit...for Paul clearly knew that all believers have the Spirit living in them from the moment of their belief...(Romans 8:9). The literal translation of Paul's question is, 'Having believed, did you receive the Holy Spirit?' 'Having believed'...is an aorist participle, which normally indicates action prior to the action of the main verb (in this case 'receive'). Thus we may render this 'Did you receive the Holy Spirit after you believed?'... Paul's question here indicates that he thought it quite possible to 'believe' in Christ without experiencing the baptism in the Holy Spirit. There is strong evidence in this passage that one may believe in Christ as a Christian without having experienced the fullness of the Holy Spirit..."[8]

4. _Some have wrongly been told that you might not receive the real thing._

They have been told that you might not receive the real thing. Jesus very clearly illustrated that this would not happen. Jesus said that if we come seeking the real thing, we will receive the real thing. Jesus said,

> *"If a son asks for bread from any father among you, will he give him a stone. Or if he asks for a fish, will he give him a serpent instead of a fish? Or if he asks for an egg, will he offer him a scorpion? If you then, being evil, know how to give good gifts to your children, how much more will your heavenly Father give the Holy Spirit to those who ask Him!"* (Luke 11:11-13 NKJV).

If we come asking for the real thing, we will receive the real thing. If faulty human parents will meet the real needs of their children instead of deceiving them with harmful gifts – how much more can we expect our heavenly Father to bless us with the real gift of the Holy Spirit.

5. _Some have wrongly been told that you will automatically receive the baptism in the Holy Spirit._

The Holy Spirit that dwells within every believer automatically comes and dwells within every believer the moment they become a believer. This we don't have to ask for.

The baptism in the Holy Spirit; however, does not automatically come into each believer. The baptism in the Holy Spirit is not forced upon anyone by God. That's why Jesus said in the previous verses,

"....how much more will your heavenly Father give the Holy Spirit to those who ask Him!" (Luke 11:13 NKJV).

If a person wants to be baptized in the Holy Spirit, he needs to ask. He needs to desire.

This also is how we know Jesus is speaking about the baptism in the Holy Spirit in this portion of scripture. If He were speaking of the Holy Spirit that dwells within every believer at salvation, He would not have said, "... how much more will your heavenly Father give the Holy Spirit to those who ask Him." The Holy Spirit automatically comes and dwells within a believer the moment they become a believer. The baptism in the Holy Spirit does not automatically come. We need to ask.

SUMMARY

Every person who has ever become a believer, a Christ-follower, was drawn to Christ by the Holy Spirit. Every believer, every follower of Christ, has the Holy Spirit dwelling in them from the moment they accept Christ. Every believer can receive the baptism in the Holy Spirit, that extra dimension of the working of the Holy Spirit.

REVIEW AND DISCUSSION QUESTIONS

1. How does the Holy Spirit draw people to Christ?
2. What happens when we pray for pre-believers?
3. How does the Holy Spirit help believers?
4. Give some examples of how the Holy Spirit has helped you.
5. What are five common misconceptions regarding the baptism in the Holy Spirit?

Chapter Two

DON'T LEAVE HOME WITHOUT IT

Some years ago there was a very popular commercial on television for the American Express credit card. In the commercial Karl Malden, a well-known actor, came on the screen and told of all the benefits of having an American Express card. Then at the end of the commercial he held up the American Express card and said these words that the commercial was famous for, "And don't leave home without it!"

In a sense, this is what Jesus was telling His disciples regarding the baptism in the Holy Spirit. Don't leave without this!

Why was this so important to Jesus? Why did Jesus feel this was so important that the disciples were not to leave without this? One preacher said, "The message of Gethsemane and Calvary had to wait for Pentecost. The transfiguration, the cross, the blood and the resurrection could not project the gospel. They had to wait for Pentecost." Why was this so important to Jesus?

Why was this so important to the Early Church? We read in Acts 8:5-25 where Philip went down to Samaria to preach about Jesus and many believed what Philip was preaching, and they accepted Christ. When the Early Church leaders in Jerusalem heard that now there were all these new believers in Samaria, the Early Church leaders took Peter and John away from whatever they were doing in Jerusalem and sent them thirty-five miles down to Samaria to tell these new believers about the baptism in the Holy Spirit. We learn from this account that:

1. <u>The Early Church thought this was important.</u> I don't know what Peter and John were doing, but whatever it was, in the eyes of the Early Church leaders it was not as important as their going down to Jerusalem to tell these new believers about the baptism in the Holy Spirit. They didn't wait and hope that somehow these new believers would hear about the baptism in the Holy Spirit. They thought this was so important that they sent Peter and John down to Samaria to tell these new believers about this. To the Early Church, this was important!

2. <u>The Early Church thought this was normal.</u> To the Early Church, this wasn't thought of as being strange or unusual. This was just normal Christianity. People come to Christ, let's tell them about the baptism in the Holy Spirit. They didn't believe this was only for some, only for a few or only for select believers. They believed this was normal for all believers.

3. <u>The Early Church did not believe there was a probationary period.</u> The Early Church didn't believe you had to be a believer for a certain period of time before you could receive the baptism in the Holy Spirit. They didn't believe you had to first prove yourself over a period of time or that you had to first arrive at a certain level of maturity. This was available as soon as someone became a believer. They sent Peter and John to Samaria as soon as they heard there were all these new believers there.

4. <u>The Early Church believed this was a gift available for all believers.</u> The Early Church did not believe the baptism in the Holy Spirit was something to be earned or merited. The Early Church didn't believe the baptism in the Holy Spirit was a merit badge or an achievement award we receive when we arrive at a certain level of holiness. These were new believers. They hadn't had a chance to get everything in order in their lives. The baptism in the Holy Spirit was not something they cleaned themselves up enough in order to receive. This was a gift that was available to every believer and the baptism in the Holy Spirit would help someone live the life Jesus desired them to live. The only qualification was to be a believer. If someone is a believer, he's eligible!

5. <u>The Early Church believed that there was a visible, physical initial sign showing someone had been baptized in the Holy Spirit.</u> What was that initial, visible, physical sign? The person would speak in a language he had not learned. He would speak in other tongues. We find this repeatedly mentioned in the book of Acts.

"And they were all filled with the Holy Spirit and began to speak with other tongues as the Spirit gave them utterance." (Acts 2:4 NKJV).

"...the gift of the Holy Spirit had been poured out on the Gentiles also. For they heard them speak with tongues..." (Acts 10:45-46 NKJV).

"And when Paul had laid hands on them, the Holy Spirit came upon them, and they spoke with tongues..." (Acts 19:6 NKJV).

In the account in Acts 8, we read where Simon saw people getting baptized in the Holy Spirit.

"When Simon saw that the Spirit was given..." (Acts 8:18 NIV).

He saw initial physical evidence that these people were getting baptized in the Holy Spirit. What did he see? When you compare this with the other examples from scripture, he would have witnessed people speaking in other tongues. The Early Church believed there was a visible, initial physical sign showing someone had been baptized in the Holy Spirit. The notes in the NIV Life in the Spirit Study Bible say regarding this passage, "This manifestation gave both the Samaritans and the apostles a verifiable sign that the Holy Spirit had come upon the new believers."[1] Evidence that they had received the baptism in the Holy Spirit.

In Acts chapter 10 we read where Peter went to Cornelius' house, and the people gathered there received the baptism in the Holy Spirit.

"The circumcised believers who had come with Peter were astonished that the gift of the Holy Spirit had been poured out even on the Gentiles. For they heard them speaking in tongues..." (Acts 10:45-46 NIV).

Peter and those with him considered speaking in tongues through the spirit as the convincing sign of the baptism in the Holy Spirit.[2]

In Acts chapter 11 Peter is explaining to the Early Church leaders what had happened at Cornelius' house and how the people had received the baptism in the Holy Spirit and began to speak in tongues. Peter said,

"As I began to speak, the Holy Spirit came upon them as he had come on us at the beginning. Then I remembered what the Lord had said: 'John baptized with water, but you shall be baptized with the Holy Spirit'" (Acts 11:15-16 NIV).

The Early Church leaders upon hearing that they spoke in tongues accepted that as the evidence that they had been baptized in the Holy Spirit. Commenting on this passage the notes in the Life in the Spirit Study Bible state, "Baptism in the Spirit should not be assumed today if...speaking in tongues are absent; nowhere in Acts is the baptism in the Holy Spirit considered an experience to be known by faith-perception alone..."[3]

Then Peter concluded by saying,

"So if God gave them the same gift as he gave us, who believed in the Lord Jesus Christ, who was I to think that I could oppose God?" (Acts 11:17 NIV).

The term "us who believed" is a Greek aorist participle, normally describing action occurring before that of the main verb. Thus, a more literal translation would be "God gave them the same gift as he gave us also after believing."[4]

The response of the Early Church leaders was,

"When they heard this, they had no further objections and praised God..." (Acts 11:18 NIV).

"Peter's speech silenced all objections. God had baptized the Gentiles with the Holy Spirit and accompanying this was the convincing evidence that they had spoken in other tongues. This was the only sign that was needed, and it was accepted without doubt."[5]

In Acts chapter 15 we see Peter before the apostles and elders explaining how the gospel message had gone out to the Gentiles through him and how they had believed and had also received the baptism in the Holy Spirit just like the apostles and elders had when they began to speak in tongues. The apostles and elders accepted this as evidence that they had received the baptism in the Holy Spirit.

The Early Church believed there was a visible, initial physical sign showing someone had been baptized in the Holy Spirit.

6. <u>The Early Church did not believe these believers were already baptized in the Holy Spirit.</u> Just because they were believers did not mean they were baptized in the Holy Spirit. This was a separate experience that was available to all believers after salvation.

WHY IS THE BAPTISM IN THE HOLY SPIRIT IMPORTANT?

The baptism in the Holy Spirit was promised by Jesus

If Jesus promised this, then this is important. If someone promises something then it's important to them, especially when it's their last words and time is short and words have to be chosen carefully. When Jesus was getting ready to ascend to heaven, He spoke about the baptism in the Holy Spirit. Why? Because Jesus saw this as being important! When Paul came across the believers in Ephesus in Acts 19, he asked if they had received the baptism in the Holy Spirit since they believed. Why did Paul ask this? Because if Jesus saw this as being important, Paul also saw this as being important. If Jesus and Paul saw this as being important, shouldn't we? This is important because this was promised by Jesus.

The baptism in the Holy Spirit was commanded by Jesus

Jesus commanded His disciples to wait in Jerusalem until they had received the baptism in the Holy Spirit.

This was not a suggestion by Jesus to His disciples, this was a command. This was so important that they were not to start without this. If Jesus saw this as being so important that He would command His disciples to not leave Jerusalem without this, shouldn't we see this as being important also?

The baptism in the Holy Spirit is immensely helpful

Jesus saw this as being so immensely helpful that the disciples were not to start without this. Paul also saw this as being so immensely helpful to the disciples in Ephesus that the first question he asked them was, if they had received the baptism in the Holy Spirit (Acts 19:2). Doctor George O. Wood commenting on this portion of scripture said, "Paul knew that, if the church at Ephesus was to grow and have a powerful impact on the city, it had to start, as did the Jerusalem church, with the template of Spirit-baptized believers."[6]

HOW IS THE BAPTISM IN
THE HOLY SPIRIT HELPFUL?

The Baptism in the Holy Spirit Helps with Power

Jesus said,

> *"But you shall receive power when the Holy Spirit has come upon you; and you shall be witnesses to Me in Jerusalem, and in all Judea and Samaria, and to the end of the earth"* (Acts 1:8 NKJV).

The word that is translated as "power" is the Greek word "dunamis" which literally means "ability" or "enablement." The baptism in the Holy Spirit gives us the power, the ability, the enablement—

- **to live the life that Jesus calls us to live**

    To live the life we are called to live as followers of Christ regardless of the circumstances or conditions.

- **to proclaim the message of Jesus Christ**

    Peter walked with Jesus for three and a half years; saw all Jesus did, heard all Jesus said, but prior to being baptized in the Holy Spirit in Acts 2; on the night when Jesus was arrested, when Peter was confronted by servant girls he denied Christ three times. After being baptized in the Holy Spirit, this same Peter was then publicly and powerfully preaching before thousands. What made the difference? The difference was he was baptized in the Holy Spirit! What's the conclusion we can draw? The Baptism in the Holy spirit did what walking side by side with Jesus for three and a half years could not accomplish. After the baptism in the Holy Spirit he publicly and powerfully proclaimed the message of Jesus.

- **to follow Jesus**

    To follow Jesus in spite of whatever opposition may come. As we look at the Early Church, we see that many times and in many places they faced opposition but they continued to follow Jesus.

- **to endure**

  To endure whatever hardships may come. Many times the Early Church faced hardships of various kinds, but they endured and continued to follow Jesus.

- **to say "no"**

  To say "no" to the temptations of sin.

- **to handle when God says "no"**

  There are times when God will say "no" and the baptism in the Holy Spirit will help us handle those times. For example, in II Corinthians 12:7-10 when Paul asked God to remove a thorn in his flesh. Three times he asked, but the Lord said "no." There also was the time in Acts 16:6-9 when Paul and his missionary party were going to go to Asia to minister, but they were forbidden by the Lord.

Today the baptism in the Holy Spirit helps us with power in these same ways. With the power to live the life Jesus calls us to live, with the power to proclaim the message of Christ, with the power to follow, with the power to endure, with the power to say "no" to sin and with the power to handle when God says "no."

The baptism in the Holy Spirit enables us to stand strong, to be what Jesus wants us to be and to do what Jesus wants us to do.

I remember reading an illustration that pictured it this way. You could go to a local fast food restaurant and pick up a soda straw at their soda counter and give it to a young child. That child could bend the soda straw with no effort or energy. If you were to take the same soda straw, bring it to a hardware store and buy a nail that was as long as a soda straw and as thick as a soda straw and insert the nail down into the soda straw, probably the strongest man in that store wouldn't be able to bend the soda straw with the nail inserted into it. That's what the baptism in the Holy Spirit does for the follower of Jesus. The baptism in the Holy Spirit enables us to stand strong, to be what Jesus wants us to be and to do what Jesus wants us to do.

Charles Crabtree, the former Assistant Superintendent of the Assemblies of God, illustrated it this way at an evangelist's conference Beth and I attended. He said, "The baptism in the Holy Spirit is like putting a strong man into the body of a 90-pound weakling."

Doctor George Wood, General Superintendent of the Assemblies of God, tells of how he was preaching in a large Assemblies of God church in a Middle Eastern country. When the building emptied of believers, the pastor explained to Dr. Wood that hundreds of Muslims were at that moment gathering outside waiting for the doors to reopen. Why were they coming? Because they knew the Christians prayed for the sick and cast out demons. Doctor Wood said, "In that church, the question of whether we need or do not need the baptism in the Holy Spirit does not even come up. When you are confronting powerful, evil forces; invading hostile, enemy territory; confronting situations individuals have no human answers for; and where positive thinking and self-help techniques do not work — you must have a power that comes from God."[7]

The baptism in the Holy Spirit helps with power.

The Baptism in the Holy Spirit Helps with Prayer

When we are baptized in the Holy Spirit, we have a whole new dimension to prayer. We can now pray in the Spirit. We can pray in a language we have not learned. We can pray in our "prayer language." It adds a whole new dimension to prayer.

Paul said,

"And pray in the Spirit on all occasions with all kinds of prayers and requests..." (Ephesians 6:18 NIV).

"...I will pray with the Spirit, and I will also pray with the understanding..." (I Corinthians 14:15 NKJV).

"Likewise the Spirit also helps in our weaknesses. For we do not know what we should pray for as we ought, but the Spirit Himself makes intercession for us with groaning's which cannot be uttered" (Romans 8:26 NKJV).

John B. McGarvey illustrated it this way:

"One day our church copy machine broke down. I'm not mechanically minded, but I called the repair shop to see if they could tell me what the problem was and if I could do anything about it. I quickly discovered, however, that I didn't even know how to describe what was broken. I didn't know the names of the parts or what was specifically wrong. I just knew the copy machine didn't work. So the repair shop sent out a technician. While working on our machine, he also called the shop. Unlike me, he knew how to describe what was needed. He used words I didn't understand, but the person at the shop did, and soon the copier was repaired. My need was met because someone came and communicated to headquarters in words that I could not express. The Apostle Paul teaches in Romans 8 that this is what the Holy Spirit does for us. When we don't know how to pray, the Holy Spirit knows precisely what we need and prays in a language the Father perfectly understands."[8]

Later in this book, we will have an entire chapter devoted to what happens when we pray in the Holy Spirit.

The Baptism in the Holy Spirit Helps with Praise

When we are baptized in the Holy Spirit, we also have a whole new dimension of praise available to us. We can praise and worship Him with our native language, but we can also praise and worship Him in the Spirit, in our unlearned language.

Paul said,

"....I will sing with the spirit, I will sing with the understanding" (I Corinthians 14:15 NKJV).

In a later chapter, we will further elaborate on this.

SUMMARY

The baptism in the Holy Spirit is important because:

- the baptism in the Holy Spirit is promised by Jesus
- the baptism in the Holy Spirit is commanded by Jesus
- the baptism in the Holy Spirit is helpful according to Jesus

REVIEW AND DISCUSSION QUESTIONS

1. What did the Early Church believe regarding the baptism in the Holy Spirit?

2. Why is the baptism in the Holy Spirit important?

3. In what six ways does the baptism in the Holy Spirit empower the life of a believer?

4. Name three ways that the baptism in the Holy Spirit is helpful in the life of a believer?

Chapter Three

BAPTIZED IN
THE HOLY SPIRIT

I remember a Sunday in our second pastorate when a family visited our church for the very first time. As they were leaving after the service they were so excited and said how much they had enjoyed the service but they said they had never been to an Assemblies of God church before and they had some questions they would like to ask. They asked if they could come in the next morning and ask their questions. I said, "Sure" and we set up a time for them to come to the office on Monday to ask their questions.

On Monday morning as the time of their appointment drew near I looked out my office window and saw them walking up the circle drive toward the front doors of the church. Just about the time they reached the front doors of the church, my phone rang. It was my mother.

My parents were both from Finland, and all of our conversations were always in Finnish. I began conversing with my mother in Finnish. In the meantime, the couple entered the lobby area of the church, and they could hear through the office wall that I was on the phone. I knew they were waiting for me so I brought the conversation with my mother to a close and then opened the office door and invited the couple to come in.

As they walked into the office that morning, they had a look of wonderment on their faces as they walked in and the husband asked, "Can I ask you a question?" I said, "Sure, that's why you came in this morning was to ask questions." He said, "Oh no pastor, I now have a new question. Was that speaking in tongues that I heard in here?" I said, "Oh no, that was just speaking in Finnish, but we do believe in the baptism in the Holy Spirit and speaking in tongues."

Sometimes the baptism in the Holy Spirit can be as new to people as it was to that couple that morning. It was to me!

TESTIMONY OF MY PERSONAL PENTECOST

I was not brought up in a Pentecostal, Charismatic or Assemblies of God church so this baptism in the Holy Spirit "stuff" was all brand new to me.

I spent the first eight years of my life in a liturgical church. My first eight years were spent attending a Lutheran church. They were wonderful, kind, loving, gracious people but during those eight years, I don't ever remember hearing them talk about the baptism in the Holy Spirit. No one ever mentioned the baptism in the Holy Spirit. No one ever talked about the baptism in the Holy Spirit.

I spent the next eight years of my life in an evangelical church. Those eight years were spent in a Baptist church. They were wonderful people who loved Jesus and endeavored to live for Him and serve Him. I will forever be grateful to them for it was during that eight-year period when at the age of ten, I made a commitment of my life to Christ. It's the greatest decision I have ever made.

I can remember hearing them talk about the baptism in the Holy Spirit. In that particular Baptist church, they believed that the baptism in the Holy Spirit that was in the Book of Acts was real and powerful. They believed the baptism in the Holy Spirit was real back then. That it was powerful back then. But they also believed that when the Book of Acts ended, so did the baptism in the Holy Spirit. They believed it was for back then and that today you receive all that you are going to receive at the time of salvation. So during those years I didn't see people receive the baptism in the Holy Spirit, and I didn't desire the baptism in the Holy Spirit after I made a commitment of my life to Christ because I was told this was not for today.

Then in my late teenage years, my parents started to attend an Assemblies of God church, and I heard about the baptism in the Holy Spirit.

As we continued to go to that church, I learned about the baptism in the Holy Spirit. I learned that this had not ended with the Book of Acts like I had been told all those years and that this was still for today.

I learned that Peter said,

"For the promise is to you and to your children, and to all who are afar off, as many as the Lord our God will call" (Acts 2:39 NKJV).

As we continued to attend that church, I began to be open to the baptism in the Holy Spirit. I began to believe that the baptism in the Holy Spirit is real, is for today and that it was nice that those people who had this had received it.

Then as we continued to attend that church, I began to casually desire the baptism in the Holy Spirit. Believing that the baptism in the Holy Spirit is real, is for today and that if the Lord wanted to hit me with this that would be fine with me. Casually desiring but not seeking. With that mindset the chances of receiving are minimal.

Jesus said,

"....how much more will your heavenly Father give the Holy Spirit to those who ask Him!" (Luke 11:13 NKJV).

Notice we need to ask. Some today have the mistaken mindset that if God wants me to have the baptism in the Holy Spirit, then it will just happen. No, we need to ask!

Then I reached the point where I really wanted to get baptized in the Holy Spirit. I kind of went through a five-step process where

- I heard about the baptism in the Holy Spirit
- I learned about the baptism in the Holy Spirit
- I became open to the baptism in the Holy Spirit
- I casually desired the baptism in the Holy Spirit

- I desperately yearned for the baptism in the Holy Spirit

I remember being prayed for at church to receive the baptism in the Holy Spirit. Do you know what happened? Nothing! Absolutely nothing! There was a reason why nothing happened which I will tell you about later in the book.

I then thought I'll pray on my own to receive the baptism in the Holy Spirit. Still, nothing happened.

By then I was in my junior year at Northern Michigan University, a secular university in Marquette, MI., majoring in business. I remember this night as vividly as if it happened last night even though it was decades ago. I had been in the college library studying until midnight, and the library was closing. I had to leave the library and walk across campus to my dormitory. There was an empty, vacant field between the library and my dormitory. As I left the library, it was the middle of the night and no one was around, so as I started walking across that empty vacant field, I began to pray out loud, "Lord, baptize me in the Holy Spirit," "Lord, I want all that you have promised," and "Lord I want all that's available."

As I was praying out loud in that field in the middle of the night, before I even fully realized what had happened, I found I wasn't praying in English any longer, but I was praying in a language I had not learned. I was speaking in a language I did not know. I was speaking in tongues!

I was baptized in the Holy Spirit walking across a field in the middle of the night at a secular university. If it can happen there, it can happen anywhere!

There were three things that caused me to desire to be baptized in the Holy Spirit.

First, I came to the conclusion that if Jesus thought this was important, then I wanted it.

Second, I came to the conclusion that if there was more available than what I had already received, then I wanted all that was available.

Third, I came to the conclusion that if the baptism in the Holy Spirit can do everything the Bible said it can, and everything people had told me it can, then I wanted and needed the baptism in the Holy Spirit.

REVOLUTIONIZED CHRISTIAN LIFE

The baptism in the Holy Spirit revolutionized my Christian life.

I Found a New Power

After I had been baptized in the Holy Spirit, I found a new power in my Christian life. People often assume that because I'm an evangelist and a former pastor that I just came out of the womb loving to speak in front of people. Let me tell you the way it really was.

I was one of those people who could not give a book report in school. I was one of those people who could not give a speech in school. Any day that I had to give a speech or book report, my stomach would be tied up in knots from nervousness. It was pitiful.

As a child the worst time of the year for me was Christmas time. It didn't matter if you were part of the

Lutheran Church, the Baptist Church or the Assemblies of God; every one of them would have those dreaded Christmas programs, and nothing short of death or the rapture would deliver you from a church Christmas program. I discovered a secret, however. Each year when they would ask who would like to be a shepherd, I would volunteer. The shepherds never said anything! I just walked around with a staff.

After I was baptized in the Holy Spirit, however; I found a new power in my life. I won't lie to you or deceive you and tell you that once you are baptized in the Holy Spirit you'll never have any fears or butterflies. That's not true. You may find that you have fears and butterflies, but you will also have a power that helps you rise above emotions and do whatever it is that Jesus wants you to do.

Jesus wasn't fooling when He said,

> *"But you shall receive power when the Holy Spirit has come upon you..."* (Acts 1:8 NKJV).

I found a new power in my life.

I Found a New Way to Pray

I found that I could now not only pray in my learned language, but I could also pray in the Spirit, in that unlearned language. Paul said,

> *"...I will pray with the Spirit, and I will also pray with the understanding..."* (I Corinthians 14:15 NKJV).

I now had a whole new dimension to my prayer life. In a later chapter, we'll discuss all that happens when we pray in the Spirit.

I Found a New Way to Build Myself Up Spiritually

I found a new way to charge my "spiritual batteries." Jude said,

"But you beloved, building yourselves up on your most holy faith, praying in the Holy Spirit" (Jude 20 NKJV).

I Found a New Way to Worship God

In addition to worshipping God in my learned language, I could worship in the Spirit. Paul said,

"...I will sing with the Spirit, and I will also sing with the understanding" (I Corinthians 14:15 NKJV).

Being baptized in the Holy Spirit revolutionized my Christian life.

SUMMARY

Regardless of one's background, the baptism in the Holy Spirit is available for all believers and can revolutionize their Christian life.

REVIEW AND DISCUSSION QUESTIONS

1. What is your spiritual background?

2. What were you taught regarding the baptism in the Holy Spirit?

3. What conclusions regarding the baptism in the Holy Spirit did the author come to?

4. How did the baptism in the Holy Spirit revolutionize the author's life?

5. If you have been baptized in the Holy Spirit, how has the baptism in the Holy Spirit changed your Christian life?

Chapter Four

INSIGHTS INTO RECEIVING THE BAPTISM IN THE HOLY SPIRIT

While any believer can be baptized in the Holy Spirit, and there is no set formula for being baptized in the Holy Spirit, there are certain things we can do to create an openness that makes it easier to receive. Jesus wants to baptize every believer in the Holy Spirit. He wants to baptize us in the Holy Spirit even more than we want to be baptized in the Holy Spirit. Sometimes we, however; can make it very difficult for Him to do what He can do very easily, so very quickly and so very much desires to do. I know because I did things that hindered me from being baptized in the Holy Spirit when I was first prayed for. Here are some requirements and some things we can do to create an openness that makes it easier to receive the baptism in the Holy Spirit.

You Must Be a Believer

The baptism in the Holy Spirit is for followers of Christ only. Also, contrary to what some would teach, the baptism in the Holy Spirit is not necessary for salvation. We find a basis for this in scripture. For example, Paul asked the disciples in Acts 19 if they had received the baptism in the Holy Spirit since they believed. They were already considered believers and baptism in the Holy Spirit was an additional separate experience that could bring huge benefits to their lives, but it was not a prerequisite to salvation. The same was true with Jesus' original disciples. They were already disciples prior to Pentecost, and the baptism in the Holy Spirit was a separate, additional experience that brought huge additional benefits to their lives.

We are saved through a commitment of our life to Christ. Period! Nothing more, nothing in addition to. We are saved simply through a commitment of our life to Christ.

You Should Believe in the Baptism in the Holy Spirit

The reason we said "should" is that in rare instances believers have received the baptism in the Holy Spirit and began speaking in tongues without even knowing what it was, let alone believing in it. This, however, is the exception and not the rule. I think in those cases, God sees the hunger in their hearts for more of Him and baptizes them in the Holy Spirit even though they don't even know about the baptism in the Holy Spirit.

You Should Desire the Baptism in the Holy Spirit

Again the reason we said "should" is because on rare occasions people have been baptized in the Holy Spirit who were not asking or seeking the baptism in the Holy Spirit. This again is the exception and not the general rule. I think in those cases, as previously mentioned, God sees the hunger in their hearts for more of Him and He baptizes them in the Holy Spirit even if they weren't asking specifically for it. Generally, however; a person must be seeking, desiring and asking for the baptism in the Holy Spirit. That's why Jesus said,

> *"...how much more will your heavenly Father give the Holy Spirit to those who ask Him!"* (Luke 11:13 NKJV).

You Should Believe Jesus Wants to Baptize You in the Holy Spirit

We should come in faith believing, expecting to be baptized in the Holy Spirit. The reason we said "should" however is that people have come forward on occasion in our services desiring to receive the baptism in the Holy Spirit but in their hearts doubting they would receive. Some perhaps have sought for a long time, have come up for prayer many times before and have not received so they think this time will most likely be no different. In spite of their doubts, however; they end up receiving the baptism in the Holy Spirit. That again, however, is the exception and not the rule. A person should come believing and expecting to be baptized in the Holy Spirit.

Begin To Praise and Worship the Lord Out Loud in Your Learned Language

The Bible tells us that in the Upper Room on the Day of Pentecost, they were praying. Part of praying is praising and worshipping God for who He is. We encourage people to close their eyes, lift their hands and begin to worship God out loud. The closing of our eyes eliminates the distractions around us. The lifting of our hands is a position of submission and surrender to God. The reason we encourage people to praise and worship the Lord out loud is that it gets their mouths open, their tongues moving, and their voices engaged so God can then fill their mouths with that unlearned language.

In the Book of Acts when describing the outpouring of the Holy Spirit on the Day of Pentecost, the Bible says,

> *"...they began to speak with other tongues as the Spirit gave them utterance..."* (Acts 2:4 KJV).

Notice the word "they." Who spoke? It was not God. It was not angels. It was "they." They spoke. God gave them the words in that unlearned language but it was "they" who spoke. In order to speak, what do we have to do? We have to open our mouths, move our tongues and put our voices to it. Without this, we will not speak English or that unlearned language.

I was prayed for in church to receive the baptism in the Holy Spirit but nothing happened. God wanted me to be baptized in the Holy Spirit. He wanted to do it even more than I wanted to receive it, but my mouth was shut and my teeth were clenched. A carpenter couldn't have gotten my mouth open with a crowbar.

A few weeks later I was baptized in the Holy Spirit walking across a field in the middle of the night at Northern Michigan University. What was the difference? While walking across that field, I was praying out loud. My mouth was already open. My tongue was already moving. My voice was already engaged. The baptism in the Holy Spirit happened quickly and easily.

The simple principle is this. If we don't open our mouths, move our tongues and engage our voices we won't speak anything; including the unlearned language that God wants to give us as the initial physical evidence of being baptized in the Holy Spirit.

Another simple principle is this. No one can speak two languages at the same time. A person cannot speak in their learned language and an unlearned language at the same time. It's one language coming out of one mouth at one time. Sometimes when praying for people, we have to get them to stop praying and praising in English so they can begin to speak in that unlearned language. Often we'll tell people "now stop the English, take a deep breath, take another deep breath, now let that unlearned language come out," and "now begin to speak in that unlearned language." And they'll begin to speak in that unlearned language, to speak in tongues.

I remember hearing an old-time Pentecostal preacher say there are only two reasons why a believer who desires to be baptized in the Holy Spirit will not be baptized in the Holy Spirit (1) a lack of faith — they don't believe they can be baptized in the Holy Spirit or (2) lack of yieldedness — they fail to yield their mouth, tongue and voice to speak the unlearned language the Holy Spirit is giving them.

We could perhaps add (3) a lack of doing our part — they are waiting for God to speak when in reality we have to speak. We have to open our mouths, move our tongues, and engage our voices. God will not force us to speak. We do the speaking. He gives us the words. If we do our part, God will do His part.

We tell believers who come to the altar seeking the baptism in the Holy Spirit there is no reason for them not to get baptized in the Holy Spirit. If they are open, hungry and desirous and will do their part; God will do His!

SUMMARY

Jesus wants to baptize His followers in the Holy Spirit even more than believers want to receive the baptism in the Holy Spirit. He knows what the baptism in the Holy Spirit can do in their lives. We, on the other hand, can make it very difficult for Him. We don't do it on purpose but unintentionally we can make it difficult. If we will remove the hindrances, we will be baptized in the Holy Spirit.

REVIEW AND DISCUSSION QUESTIONS

1. What is the non-negotiable requirement to being baptized in the Holy Spirit?

2. Is the baptism in the Holy Spirit necessary for salvation?

3. What are some hindrances to receiving the baptism in the Holy Spirit?

4. What hindered the author from getting baptized in the Holy Spirit?

5. How do we overcome the hindrances to being baptized in the Holy Spirit?

Chapter Five

NOW WHAT?

After a person accepts Christ, we give them follow-up instructions to help them understand what they have done, what they now have, what they should now do and how to not allow the enemy to steal from them what they have received.

It's just as important for us to share follow-up instructions with those who have just been baptized in the Holy Spirit. Telling them what they now have, how to put to use what they have received and how to make sure the enemy does not confuse them or steal from them what they have received.

When I was baptized in the Holy Spirit while walking across a field alone at Northern Michigan University, there was no one around to share with me what I'm about to share with you. The enemy deceived me into thinking I had made it all up, that it wasn't real and that it wasn't from God. It wasn't until later when a Spirit-filled believer shared with me some of the things I'm about to share with you that I realized I had been deceived by the enemy.

In order to prevent others from making the same mistake I did, I always share these five basic follow-up points with those who have been baptized in the Holy Spirit, whether it's at an altar at the end of one of our services with a group of people or it's one on one.

Don't Let Anyone Talk You Out of What You Have Experienced

If you spoke in an unlearned language, you were baptized in the Holy Spirit! Period! Don't let the devil talk you out of it. He will try. He will tell you, "that wasn't God, that was you, you made all that up." He did it to me, and he'll try to do it to you. I believed him until a Spirit-filled believer pulled me aside and told me I had been fooled by the enemy. Don't make the same mistake I did! Oh yes, we opened our mouths, we moved our tongues, and we put a voice to it because we won't speak anything if we don't open our mouths, move our tongues and put a voice to it. But it was God who gave us those words we had not learned. It was God who gave us those words in that unlearned language. Don't let the devil talk you out of your baptism in the Holy Spirit.

Also, don't let your friends talk you out of what you have received. Not every believer in Christ believes in the baptism in the Holy Spirit. If you have friends who don't believe in the baptism in the Holy Spirit, and they don't want to believe in it, then that's their loss. Hang on to what you have received. Don't let them talk you out of your baptism in the Holy Spirit.

Finally, don't talk yourself out of what you have received. Don't say to yourself, "I don't know if anything happened." If you were speaking in an unlearned language, something happened! You were baptized in the Holy Spirit!

Don't let anyone talk you out of what you have received. Not the devil, not other people and not yourself.

Don't Base the Reality of Your Experience on What You Did or Did Not Feel

As we pointed out earlier, everyone who is baptized in the Holy Spirit will initially speak in an unlearned language. It's the initial physical evidence. In addition to speaking in an unlearned language, some people have tears coming down their cheeks. Some feel warm and fuzzy all over. Others feel great joy. Some feel like they are ready to explode. Others may feel like the lady who called her pastor up in the middle of the night and asked, "How do you shut this thing off?"

On the other hand, the night I was baptized in the Holy Spirit walking across the field in the middle of the night, in addition to speaking in an unlearned language, my reaction was, "Oh that was nice." There were no tears, no overwhelming ecstatic feeling. Just, "Oh, that was nice." Was it real? It was. The initial physical evidence of the baptism in the Holy Spirit is not what a person feels! The initial physical evidence is to speak in an unlearned language.

A pastor shared this illustration regarding this point. There was a lady who at the end of a service had watched a number of people receive the baptism in the Holy Spirit. Afterward, she came up to the pastor and said, "Those people weren't baptized in the Holy Spirit. They didn't cry like I did." She was under the mistaken assumption that everyone who received the baptism in the Holy Spirit had to experience the same emotional reaction. That assumption is just as wrong as assuming everyone has to physically and emotionally respond in a certain way when they accept Christ. That everyone would have to get knocked off a horse when they come to Christ like Saul (Paul) did when he came to Christ.

We encourage people to not compare their experience in receiving the baptism in the Holy Spirit with someone else's. Just be thankful for what you have received! If, in addition to speaking in an unlearned language, you had tears — great. If you felt an ecstatic feeling — great. If, on the other hand, your reaction was "that was nice," your experience was just as real. Just thank God for what you have received.

Don't base the reality of what you have experienced on what you did or did not feel. The initial physical evidence is not what a person feels but that they spoke in an unlearned language.

Put to Use Every Day What You Have Received

Everyday take time to pray in that unlearned language. People who receive the baptism in the Holy Spirit at church may ask, "Can I do this at home?" The answer is, yes! Please do this at home. Do this in the car. Do this wherever you can. You don't have to be at the church.

People also ask, "Can I start and stop this?" The answer is, yes. Paul said,

"...I will pray with the spirit, and I will also pray with the understanding..." (I Corinthians 14:15 NKJV).

Notice "I will." We can choose to pray in the Spirit. We can choose to pray in our native language. Take time to pray "in the Spirit" every day. It's powerful. We'll cover this in more detail in a later chapter.

Also, don't get hung up on how many or how few words you have in that unlearned language. Some people, when they receive the baptism in the Holy Spirit, seemingly have a whole language right away. Others have only a few words, some only one word.

We were at a church in Minnesota a while ago, and the pastor said that when he received the baptism in the Holy Spirit, he had only one word, perhaps only a one syllable word. What's wrong if we are saying "thank you" to God in an unlearned language? It doesn't take many words or syllables to say "thank you" or to say "help."

Doctor Doyle Jones said in his book *Be Filled with the Spirit* to not be concerned if only a few syllables or words come at the beginning. In Acts 10:46 when the Gentiles at Cornelius' house were baptized in the Holy Spirit the Bible says,

"...they heard them speak with tongues and magnify God..." (Acts 10:46 NKJV).

Doctor Jones goes on to say that "hallelujah, praise the Lord, thank you Jesus, and glory to God" and variations of these praise phrases show the limitations of the English language in praising God. In many other languages, the same limits exist. So it is when someone is baptized in the

Holy Spirit. They may be magnifying God in an unlearned language, and the words may seem redundant and repetitious at first.[1]

If we keep using what we have received, the words will grow into phrases. The phrases grow into sentences. The sentences become paragraphs. The paragraphs become a full language. We encourage people to use what they have received, and that language will grow. Also, on the practical side, as you are using that unlearned language, slow down. As you slowly speak those unlearned words, you will find new words forming.

Ask Questions to Learn More

We encourage people who have just received the baptism in the Holy Spirit to ask a Spirit-filled pastor if they have any questions. There are no wrong questions. We encourage them to just ask.

Embrace This Experience as a Gateway

Finally, we encourage those who have been baptized in the Holy Spirit to look at the baptism in the Holy Spirit not as an end. It is not something we check off a spiritual checklist saying, "Now I have this," and seeing this as the end. Receiving the baptism in the Holy Spirit is not an end, it's the beginning of a new dimension in our Christian life.

Doctor Gordon Anderson, president at North Central University, said in a message he preached on the Holy Spirit, that the baptism in the Holy Spirit is like going through a doorway into a new room. When we are baptized in the Holy Spirit, we gain a new power, a new way to pray, a new way to build ourselves up and a whole host of other new benefits. It's not an end but rather a beginning to a whole new dimension to our Christian life.

The only tragedy would be to walk through a doorway into a wonderful new room and then walk back out again. That's what happens if we don't put the baptism in the Holy Spirit to use in our lives by praying in the Spirit.

We also tell people that just because they are baptized in the Holy Spirit, this doesn't mean that all their old problems are gone and they will never have any new problems. We find there were plenty of problems for believers in the Book of Acts after they were baptized in the Holy Spirit in Acts 2 on the Day of Pentecost. There were all kinds of problems! But, we also see that the power they received was greater than any problem they faced. The power enabled them to face whatever problems came their way. We have that same power available to us through the baptism in the Holy Spirit.

Follow-Up Instructions for Those Who Did Not Receive

We also share follow-up instructions with those who did not receive. While most people receive the baptism in the Holy Spirit when they are prayed for, there are some who do not and we share follow-up instructions with them also, to encourage them.

First, we encourage them to not be discouraged. To know that God loves them, and He wants to baptize them in the Holy Spirit even more than they want to receive it.

Second, we encourage them to keep seeking. To stay open, stay hungry. To keep praying, keep desiring to be baptized in the Holy Spirit.

Third, we encourage them that if they will stay open, stay hungry, desiring to be baptized in the Holy Spirit; they will be baptized in the Holy Spirit. It may happen at home, in the car, in the shower, in bed or in any number of other places. We also tell people to not worry that they might suddenly burst out in an unlearned language in the checkout line at the store. It will generally happen where they are praying, open, and seeking God.

The promise to those who did not receive is that if they will stay open and stay hungry to be baptized in the Holy Spirit, they will receive the baptism in the Holy Spirit.

SUMMARY

Just as follow-up instructions are important for those who have just accepted Christ, so follow-up instructions are important and helpful for those who have just been baptized in the Holy Spirit. Without follow-up instructions, the enemy can very easily deceive them and steal from them what they have received. We need to give follow-up instructions to help them understand what has happened to them, what they have received, how they can know they have received it, and what they should do with it.

Also, follow-up instructions are important for those who did not receive. Without this encouragement, they can easily become discouraged and quit desiring to be baptized in the Holy Spirit. This would be a tragedy because God wants to baptize them in the Holy Spirit even more than they want to receive the baptism in the Holy Spirit.

Follow-up is important.

REVIEW AND DISCUSSION QUESTIONS

1. Why are follow-up instructions important for those newly baptized in the Holy Spirit?

2. What are the five basic things we should share with those who have just received the baptism in the Holy Spirit?

3. Did the Early Church experience any problems after being baptized in the Holy Spirit in Acts 2 on the Day of Pentecost?

4. What three things should we share with those who were prayed for but did not receive the baptism in the Holy Spirit?

Chapter Six

UNLEASHING THE BAPTISM IN THE HOLY SPIRIT

I remember reading about a man who needed to cut down trees on his property. He went to the local hardware store and told the salesman what his project was. The salesman brought him over to the chainsaws and told him that this particular saw would enable him to cut down a dozen trees in one day. The man bought the saw and left the store with the chainsaw under his arm and a smile on his face.

At the end of the next day, he was back at the same hardware store. The chainsaw was under his arm, but the smile was gone. He asked, "Where's the salesman who sold me this saw?"

They pointed him in the direction of the salesman. He located the salesman and said to him, "I thought you said this saw could cut down a dozen trees in one day. It took me all day to cut down one tree!"

The salesman was puzzled and asked to see the saw. He checked it out and everything seemed to be perfect. He then pulled the cord and started the chainsaw.

When he started the chainsaw, the man jumped back and exclaimed, "What's that noise?"

The man had been trying to cut down the tree without starting the saw! He had been using it like it was an old-fashioned handsaw! He didn't realize the power he had available to him.

Sometimes the same thing can happen regarding the baptism in the Holy Spirit. People have certain expectations and anticipations regarding the baptism in the Holy Spirit, but because they misunderstand what the baptism in the Holy Spirit is, they misunderstand what the baptism in the Holy Spirit will do, they don't know how to apply the baptism in the Holy Spirit to their lives. They find themselves disappointed, disillusioned, defeated, or hanging on to a doctrine they still believe but not experiencing the reality of the baptism in the Holy Spirit in their lives.

In this chapter, we're going to deal with unleashing the baptism in the Holy Spirit, but first we have to know what we can expect regarding the baptism in the Holy Spirit.

DECLARATIONS OF THE BAPTISM IN THE HOLY SPIRIT

After Jesus had been crucified, buried and resurrected; He appeared to His disciples many times during the next forty days before He ascended to heaven. As Jesus spoke to His disciples during the course of those forty days, He commanded them to not leave Jerusalem until they had received the baptism in the Holy Spirit.

Jesus said,

"I am going to send you what my Father has promised; but stay in the city until you have been clothed with power from on high." (Luke 24:49 NIV).

Jesus was telling His disciples, don't leave without this!

Then just before ascending to heaven, Jesus made three powerful declarations regarding the baptism in the Holy Spirit. As we mentioned earlier, these are His last recorded words before He ascended to heaven.

When people get down to their last words, they talk about what's important. Let's look at three powerful declarations of "you shall" Jesus made just before He ascended to heaven.

You Shall Be Baptized with the Holy Spirit

"For John truly baptized with water, but you shall be baptized with the Holy Spirit not many days from now." (Acts 1:5 NKJV)

This was the promise. This was what they were to wait for. This was why they were not to leave Jerusalem. This was so important they were not to go without this. They were not to start without this.

As we discussed earlier, they were already disciples. They already had the Holy Spirit dwelling in them in the same way every believer today has the Holy Spirit dwelling within them. This, however, was a separate, additional experience that would bring additional benefits to their lives.

The declaration and promise was, "you shall be baptized in the Holy Spirit." The promise and declaration was for them back then and it's just as real for any believer today. If a person is a believer and is open, hungry and desirous; the promise is "you shall be baptized in the Holy Spirit." If a person stays open, stays hungry and desirous of the baptism in the Holy Spirit, he will receive the baptism in the Holy Spirit!

It doesn't matter how long they have sought, how many times they have been prayed for, how many times they have prayed; if they will stay open, hungry, desirous, and continue seeking — the promise is "you shall be baptized in the Holy Spirit."

In our services, we have seen people who have sought for years receive the baptism in the Holy Spirit. The key being, they didn't give up, and they came up for prayer. They stayed open and hungry!

You Shall Receive Power

"But you shall receive power when the Holy Spirit has come upon you..." (Acts 1:8 NKJV).

Jesus declared that when we are baptized in the Holy Spirit, we receive power.

As I look back on my life, there have been pivotal turning points in my life. When I committed of my life to Christ, it was a pivotal turning point in my life. When I received the baptism in the Holy Spirit, it was a pivotal turning point in my life.

As I look back on my life, there were changes that happened in my Christian life after I was baptized in the Holy Spirit that have no explanation for them except they happened after I was baptized in the Holy Spirit. All the changes were not instantaneous, but they occurred after I was baptized in the Holy Spirit.

One change was that I found a new power in my life. Let me explain how it happened in my life because some people say, "I was baptized in the Holy Spirit, and I didn't find any power." Let me tell you perhaps why that happened by illustrating from my own life how I discovered that new power after I was baptized in the Holy Spirit.

As I mentioned in a previous chapter, I was the kind of person who could not give a book report or speech in school. On the morning of having to speak in front of the class, I would be found at home standing in front of the sink, throwing up. A short time after I had received the baptism in the Holy Spirit, the pastor of the Marquette Gospel Tabernacle, the church I attended while at Northern Michigan University, asked me if I would be willing to share my testimony on Sunday night during the Evening Service. He was referring to my testimony of salvation. He had no idea I had recently been baptized in the Holy Spirit because I was alone when I had received the baptism. I don't know what possessed him to ask me except that God was arranging things in order to teach me a valuable lesson.

When he asked me, I agreed, but I spent the rest of the week saying to myself, "Why did you say 'yes'? What were you thinking? God if you get me through this I'll never say yes to him again!"

You might be asking, "Where was the power?" I'll get to that.

Sunday night came, and I was scared. My palms were sweaty, my hands were cold, my knees were shaking, and my stomach felt like a family of butterflies had moved in. I kept hoping something would happen in the service so they would forget my part. You might say, "Where was the power?" I'm getting to that.

After the worship time, the pastor introduced me and had me come up. My palms were still sweaty, my hands were cold, my knees were still shaking and the butterflies were still there. But when I started speaking, I found there was a new power helping me to do what God had opened up the door for me to do. Were there fears? Yes. Were there butterflies? Yes. But there was also a new power helping me to rise above the butterflies to do what God wanted me to do.

A few days later the leader of Intervarsity Christian Fellowship, the Christian organization I was a part of while attending Northern Michigan University, came up to me and said the Bible Study leader would be gone next week. He asked if I would lead the Bible Study. I had never led a Bible Study in my life! I can assure you that when you can't speak in front of people, you don't have a lot of experience leading Bible Studies. I don't know what possessed him to ask me, except that God was again arranging things to reinforce what He was trying to teach me.

I agreed to lead the Bible study but again the rest of the week I was saying to myself, "Why did you say, yes?" "What were you thinking?" Once again the fears and butterflies were there. When Thursday night came,

I was nervous. My hands were sweaty. My hands were cold. My knees were shaking. The butterflies were there again. But again, I found that once I started, there was a new power helping me do what God had opened the door for me to do.

The point is, if we wait until there are no fears, we will never do anything for God! I remember hearing a preacher say at a conference I attended years ago, "I don't think I have ever done anything for God when I wasn't afraid." The power is not the absence of fear, but rather the enablement and ability to rise above the fear and go on to do whatever it is God wants us to do.

One of the greatest lessons we can learn is to go on in spite of our fears to do whatever it is that God wants us to do. As we step out, we will find the power is there. Don't let fear stop you from doing what God wants you to do.

I found a new power!

You Shall Be My Witnesses

Jesus said,

"...and you shall be witnesses to Me in Jerusalem, and in all Judea and Samaria and to the end of the earth" (Acts 1:8 NKJV).

There was a purpose for the power. That we would be witnesses for Him in our Jerusalem (in the town where we live), in our Judea (in our state), in our Samaria (to other cultures) and to the ends of the earth. The baptism in the Holy Spirit was given for a purpose. To be witnesses! The baptism in the Holy Spirit wasn't given just so we would have an experience. The baptism in the Holy Spirit wasn't given just we could say we have received this. The baptism in the Holy Spirit was given in order to give us the power to be witnesses for Christ.

What is a witness? A witness in our judicial system is someone who has seen something, heard something, or experienced something, and they share it with the court. In the same sense, a witness for Christ is someone who has seen something, heard something, or experienced something, and they share it.

In Acts 4:20 it says of the Early Church,

"For we cannot but speak the things we have seen and heard" (Acts 4:20 NKJV).

They simply spoke the things they had seen and heard, and the baptism in the Holy Spirit gave them the power, the ability, the enablement. Will there be butterflies? Yes. Will there be fears? Yes. But don't let the fears and butterflies stop you. When God opens a door, go through it and allow the baptism in the Holy Spirit give you the power to be the witness He wants you to be.

Prior to being baptized in the Holy Spirit, just the thought of witnessing to someone was enough to just about put me into cardiac arrest. I remember being challenged in a service to be a witness and being stirred in my heart to be a witness, but the thought of talking to someone about Jesus petrified me. To even hand out a tract petrified me. Then I came up with a plan where I would take some tracts to the Junior College I was attending at the time, and I would leave them in the men's bathroom by the sinks. I remember the morning I waited outside the doors of the bathroom until it looked like no one was around, then I went into the bathroom and when no one was in there I put the tracts down by the sinks and ran out of the bathroom as fast as I could go.

The funny thing is that some months later after I was baptized in the Holy Spirit, the Friday night fellowship group I was a part of on campus was going to go hand out tracts and I found I could do this. I had found a new power to be a witness.

While I was in Bible School, the church Beth and I attended had a door-to-door witnessing ministry called Evangelism Explosion, and I found I could talk to people about Jesus.

In our second pastorate, we had a ministry we called "Fishers of Men." On Saturday mornings, we would have an hour of teaching where I would teach principles regarding sharing Christ and then we would go door to door for the next two hours in teams or two or three sharing Christ. It was one of the most exciting times of the week, and the Holy Spirit gave the power, the ability, and the enablement to be the witnesses He wanted us to be.

I have often thought of how the baptism in the Holy Spirit helped me go from someone who would drop tracts on a shelf in the bathroom to someone who could share Jesus.

These were the declarations Jesus made with truth and authority!

- you shall be baptized in the Holy Spirit
- you shall receive power
- you shall be my witnesses

Notice Jesus did not say "you might" but He said, "you shall." The declarations were for the early church disciples, and they are just as real and valid for every follower of Jesus today.

DISAPPOINTED IN THE BAPTISM IN THE HOLY SPIRIT

In spite of the positive declarations of "you shall" by Jesus regarding the baptism in the Holy Spirit, you find people who have been baptized in the Holy Spirit but today find themselves disappointed, disillusioned, defeated, or hanging on to a doctrine they still believe in but don't experience as a reality in their lives.

So, what happened? Did Jesus lie? Are the "you shall" declarations not true? Did the Holy Spirit run out of power? After all, it's been over 2,000 years since Pentecost. Or, do people today receive a different baptism in the Holy Spirit than the kind Jesus promised and the kind received in that Upper Room?

No, I'm convinced what people receive today is the very same baptism in the Holy Spirit they received in that Upper Room. I'm convinced the baptism in the Holy Spirit is just as powerful today as the baptism in the Holy Spirit was in the Early Church. And I'm convinced Jesus didn't lie. The "you shall" declarations are just as true today as they were back when Jesus spoke them.

So why are some who have been baptized in the Holy Spirit disappointed, disillusioned, defeated and left hanging on to a doctrine they still believe but not experiencing the reality in their life? Let me give you four reasons.

False Expectations

Some are disappointed, disillusioned, defeated or left with only a doctrine because they expected the baptism in the Holy Spirit to do something it was never intended to do. They expected the baptism in the Holy Spirit to make all their problems go away. The baptism in the Holy Spirit will affect us. The baptism in the Holy Spirit will give us new power. The baptism in the Holy Spirit will change us. It will change our power life, our prayer life, and our personal life. The baptism in the Holy Spirit will not, however, make all our problems disappear. The baptism in the Holy Spirit is not a "spiritual eraser" on the problems in life. The baptism in the Holy Spirit is not a "spiritual cocoon" that makes us immune to any future problems.

We only have to look at the Early Church and ask, "Did they have any problems after they were baptized in the Holy Spirit in Acts chapter two?" As we read through the book of Acts, we find they were beaten, they were imprisoned, they were arrested, they were falsely accused, and they had a myriad of other problems. The Book of Acts is a chronicling of problems! But the Book of Acts is also a chronicling of how the power of the baptism in the Holy Spirit was bigger than any problem they faced. Through the power of the baptism in the Holy Spirit, they were able to deal with, go through and overcome any problem they faced. And so can we!

Unused Power

Some are disappointed, disillusioned, defeated or left with only a doctrine because they don't put to use what they have received. This is why we tell people to pray in the Spirit every day. We will devote an entire chapter to this later. Paul said,

> *"...I will pray with the Spirit, I will also pray with the understanding..."* (I Corinthians 14:15 NKJV).

> *"I thank my God I speak with tongues more than you all;"* (I Corinthians 14:18 NKJV).

If we don't use what we have received, we will be disappointed.

You could buy the greatest car on the market but if you drive it home and park it in the garage and don't use it; you will be disappointed. We need to put to use what we have received.

Comparing Your Experience to Others

Some are disappointed, disillusioned, defeated or left with only a doctrine because they compare their experience in receiving to someone else's experience in receiving. As we have previously mentioned, everyone who is baptized in the Holy Spirit will initially speak in tongues, in an unlearned language. We call it, "the initial physical evidence" of the baptism in the Holy Spirit. In addition to the initial physical evidence, some people may have tears coming down their cheeks, some may feel like they have been hit with a jolt of electricity, others may feel warm and fuzzy inside. These are all great physical reactions. On the other hand, in addition to speaking in an unlearned language, someone's reaction may be like mine was, "Oh, that was nice." It's just as real, and that person is just as baptized in the Holy Spirit as the one who experienced a great physical or emotional manifestation. The initial physical evidence is speaking in an unlearned language, not a physical or emotional manifestation.

The encouragement is, don't compare your experience in receiving with someone else's experience in receiving. Just thank God and rejoice in what He has done and will be doing in your life!

Holding Back

Some are disappointed, disillusioned, defeated or left with only a doctrine because they don't unleash the baptism in the Holy Spirit. My father worked in an iron ore mine during my early years. One of the tools of the trade for the iron ore miner was dynamite. I learned from my father that dynamite had incredible potential power. I also learned that this incredible potential power had to be unleashed. The power was useless if it wasn't unleashed. I learned that in order for the power to be unleashed you had to have a fuse, blasting caps, and a spark. Without these, the dynamite did absolutely nothing.

I could hold a stick of dynamite in my hands. Incredible potential power but without the fuse, the blasting caps, and the spark, the dynamite did absolutely nothing to me or for me. Why wouldn't it do anything? Because the power was never unleashed.

The same thing can happen regarding the baptism in the Holy Spirit. We can have this incredible, potential power but it lies dormant within us. Why? Because the power is not unleashed. We're like someone holding a stick of dynamite in their hands, wondering why isn't this doing something. Why isn't this doing what everyone says it should do?

DEMONSTRATING THE BAPTISM IN
THE HOLY SPIRIT

So how do we unleash the baptism in the Holy Spirit? How do we demonstrate the working of the baptism in the Holy Spirit? In the spiritual sense; what are the blasting caps, the fuse, and the spark? How do we set off the effects of the baptism in the Holy Spirit in our life? Let me give you four "Ps" to unleashing the baptism in the Holy Spirit.

Personal Time with God

We unleash the baptism in the Holy Spirit by having a consistent, regular time of personal prayer, personal reading of the Bible and personal worship. We do these things in church, but we also need to do these things on a daily basis at home. Without this personal time with God, it doesn't matter if we have been baptized in the Holy Spirit, it will not be released in our life. We'll be like someone holding a stick of dynamite in their hands, wondering where the power is.

In fact, believers who have not been baptized in the Holy Spirit, but who have personal time with God each day will have more of the working of the Holy Spirit released in their lives than someone who has been baptized in the Holy Spirit but doesn't have personal time with God. Why? Because they are releasing as much of the working of the Holy Spirit as they have available.

The believers who have been baptized in the Holy Spirit, but don't spend personal time with God, have incredible potential power, but it lies dormant in their lives. Why? Because it's not being unleashed.

What's the greatest combination? Be baptized in the Holy Spirit and spend personal time with God. That's explosive! That's Early Church Christianity.

After the Early Church was baptized in the Holy Spirit in Acts 2, did they individually quit spending time with God? No! They spent time in prayer. They spent time in the Word. They spent time worshipping God. This personal time with God was a key to unleashing of the baptism in the Holy Spirit they received in Acts 2.

Purity

Unconfessed and unrepented sin in our lives will hinder the unleashing of the baptism in the Holy Spirit. To have unrepented sin in our lives is like soaking a stick of dynamite in water and then wondering why it doesn't work.

As a boy, I remember my dad bringing home the empty wooden boxes the dynamite was packed in. The company allowed the miners to bring the empty crates home, and we had several at our house. The boxes were about eighteen inches long, twelve inches wide, and six inches high. On the sides of the boxes it said in large letters "Danger — Explosives." It also said on the box, "Keep Dry." Dynamite didn't work well if it got wet.

I liken having unconfessed and unrepented sin in our lives to being like soaking a stick of dynamite. We must confess sin in our lives. We must ask for forgiveness of sins. We must repent of our sins. Sins prevent the unleashing of the baptism in the Holy Spirit in our lives.

Let's not excuse our sins. Let's not make provision for sins in our lives. Instead let's confess our sin, ask forgiveness for it, and repent of it to unleash the baptism in the Holy Spirit.

Purpose

As we stated earlier, the baptism in the Holy Spirit was given for a purpose. For us to be witnesses. We are to be witnesses with our words, our lives, our actions, and our reactions. The baptism in the Holy Spirit is unleashed when it is needed, when there is a purpose.

I heard this illustration at an evangelist's conference. When electricians come into a building and wire it, before they leave, they promise that there is power in the outlets. When people are baptized in the Holy Spirit, Jesus promised that they will receive power.

Jesus said,

"...you shall receive power when the Holy Spirit has come upon you..." (Acts 1:8 NKJV).

When a person is baptized in the Holy Spirit, the power is within them. Jesus promised, "You shall receive power." Just as the electrician promised there would be power in the outlets, Jesus promised the power of the baptism in the Holy Spirit is within us when we are baptized in the Holy Spirit. The power is there!

Now picture this. You can have two outlets in the same room, and the power is being released from one, and the power lies dormant in the other. They both have the power within them as the electrician promised. So what's the difference? One outlet has something plugged into it, and so the power is released. The other outlet has just as much power in it, but it lies dormant because nothing is plugged in. The power is not being released because there is no purpose for it. It's not needed. The fact that the power is not being released doesn't mean there is no power. The power is there, it's just not being released.

In the spiritual realm, the baptism in the Holy Spirit is released-unleashed-when it is needed. When there is a need. When there is a purpose.

The baptism in the Holy Spirit is like the passing gear on a car. It's there, but you don't drive around in the passing gear. But when you're cruising down the highway, and you need to pass someone, you step on the gas pedal and the passing gear kicks in. It kicks in on demand. When there's a purpose for it to kick in.

I don't sense the unleashing of the baptism in the Holy Spirit when I'm hunting or fishing. I don't need it then. I can sense the presence of God but I don't sense an unleashing of the power of the Holy Spirit then because I don't need it then. I don't sense the unleashing of the power of the baptism in the Holy Spirit when I'm sitting because I don't need it then. I can sense His presence, but I don't sense the unleashing of the power of the Holy Spirit.

I do sense the unleashing of the power of the baptism in the Holy Spirit when I'm preaching because I desperately need it then. I sense the unleashing of the power of the baptism in the Holy Spirit when I'm teaching because I desperately need it then. I sense the unleashing of the power of the baptism in the Holy Spirit when I'm witnessing because I desperately need it then. I sense the unleashing of the power of the baptism in the Holy Spirit when I'm in a time of need because I desperately need it then. It kicks in when there is a need. When there is a purpose. Like the power in an outlet. Like the passing gear on a car. It's unleashed when there is a purpose.

When we were pastoring, people would watch a fellow Spirit-filled believer go victoriously through a very difficult, trying situation. They would say to me, "I don't think I could ever go through what those people are going through." My response to them was, "I'm absolutely convinced that you could make it if you were in those circumstances. But, right now you're not in those circumstances so you're not experiencing the power, the ability, the enablement of the baptism in the Holy Spirit for those circumstances. You're on the outside looking in. They're in the middle of it, and the baptism in the Holy Spirit is giving them the power for those circumstances. If you were in the middle of those circumstances, the baptism in the Holy Spirit would be giving you the power."

Many times those same individuals would later find themselves in the same kind of circumstances and through the power of the baptism in the Holy Spirit they would make it through just fine. The baptism in the Holy Spirit kicks in when there is a need. When there is a purpose.

That's why it's futile for us to try to imagine what it would be like in a certain type of trial because we're looking at it through the eyes of the natural not realizing the power the baptism in the Holy Spirit will give us when we are in the middle of it. We don't need to fear the future but instead stay full of the Holy Spirit and desire to see the purposes of God fulfilled in and through our lives.

As we look at the Early Church, a key to the unleashing of the baptism in the Holy Spirit that they received in Acts 2 was their desire to see the purposes of God fulfilled in and through their lives.

We unleash the baptism in the Holy Spirit through purpose.

Praying in the Holy Spirit

When we pray in the Holy Spirit, it catapults our experience from the natural into the supernatural.

Jackie Pullinger, who was a missionary to Hong Kong, said she saw very little ministry success until she began to pray in the Spirit. Then she said, "He began to work, and no one works like Him".[1]

As we pray in the Spirit, we release the Holy Spirit to work.

Paul said,

"And pray in the Spirit on all occasions with all kinds of prayers and requests..." (Ephesians 6:18 NIV).

As we pray in the Spirit, we unleash the baptism in the Holy Spirit. We'll share more on this in the next chapter.

SUMMARY

Jesus said, "You shall be baptized in the Holy Spirit." If you are a believer, you are open, and you are desirous; the promise is "you shall be baptized in the Holy Spirit."

Jesus said, "You shall receive power." When you are baptized in the Holy Spirit the power is in you. It just needs to be unleashed.

Jesus said, "You shall be my witnesses." If we let Him open the doors and are willing to step out and go through them, we will be witnesses.

Everything Jesus said regarding the baptism in the Holy Spirit is true. It doesn't have to be a disappointment, a delusion, a defeat, or just a doctrine we believe.

We can unleash the baptism in the Holy Spirit through

- personal time with God
- purity
- purpose
- praying in the Holy Spirit

We will find the baptism in the Holy Spirit to be everything Jesus said it would be.

REVIEW AND DISCUSSION QUESTIONS

1. What three declarations did Jesus make just before He ascended to heaven?

2. Did all the fears leave the author's life when he was baptized in the Holy Spirit? How did he overcome the fears?

3. Why do some people who have been baptized in the Holy Spirit find themselves disappointed, disillusioned, defeated, or left with a doctrine they still believe but don't experience in their lives?

4. What are four keys to unleashing the baptism in the Holy Spirit in our lives?

5. What is the primary overall purpose for the baptism in the Holy Spirit?

Chapter Seven

PRAYING IN THE SPIRIT

A s we travel across America in ministry, we see four wheel drive vehicles. Whether it's pickup trucks or SUVs, they are everywhere. Many times on the back corner of the pickup truck it says "4 x 4" and then underneath that it will often say, "Off Road Vehicle." You've seen them. They're everywhere.

Surveys of the people who own these four-wheel drive vehicles show that 90% of them never leave the highway. Ninety percent never leave the road. Even though they were made to go off road, 90% are never put to their fullest use.

In fact a creative British company has capitalized on this fact. They have created a product called "Spray-On Mud." With this product, city dwellers can make it look like they have gone off road hunting or fishing without ever leaving town.[1]

Ninety percent of four-wheel drive vehicles are never put to their fullest use.

This same kind of thing can happen regarding the baptism in the Holy Spirit when we fail to put to fullest use what we have received. Unfortunately, what happens in many cases is that people receive the baptism in the Holy Spirit, but they fail to keep it fresh in their life. There is a world of difference between someone who *was* baptized in the Holy Spirit and someone who *is* baptized in the Holy Spirit. For one it's a memory and for the other it's a fresh up-to-date experience.

For some, it's been weeks, months or even years since they prayed in the Spirit, in that unlearned language. In fact, Pew Forum on Religion and Public Life conducted a survey on how often Pentecostals speak in tongues. The results, published in the February 18, 2007 issue of *Today's Pentecostal Evangel*, showed that 49% never speak in tongues again after they are baptized in the Holy Spirit. The survey went on to state that only 15% speak in tongues on a daily basis. The rest of the survey showed 11% do more than once a week, 7% once a week, 9% at least monthly, 2% several times a year and 6% less than several times a year.[2]

It's sad that 49% of believers never pray in the Spirit after their initial baptism in the Holy Spirit. It's sad that only 15% pray in the Spirit on a daily basis.

As we look at the Early Church, we read in Acts 4:31,

"And when they had prayed, the place where they were assembled together was shaken; and they were all filled with the Holy Spirit and they spoke the word of God with boldness" (Acts 4:31 NKJV).

When I read that portion of scripture, I take it that "they" here refers to the same ones who in Acts 2 were baptized in the Holy Spirit, and here they are being refilled, refreshed, and renewed. The bottom line is that something that isn't fresh doesn't do us any good. It may be a great memory, but it doesn't do us any good for everyday living today.

An analogy I've used is this. "You can't sail on yesterday's wind."

You and I cannot function on yesterday's infilling of the Holy Spirit today. We need a fresh infilling of the Holy Spirit today. That's why Paul said to the Ephesians,

"...be filled with the Spirit," (Ephesians 5:18 NKJV).

The Greek word that is translated "filled" literally means "to keep on being filled."

Paul knew that you and I can't fully function on yesterday's infilling of the Holy Spirit any more than you and I can sail a boat today on yesterday's wind. We need a fresh infilling of the Holy Spirit today. We miss something by not praying in the Spirit every day, by not putting to fullest use what we have available to us.

Listen to what some well-known church leaders have said regarding this issue.

John G. Lake, the great preacher, missionary, said, "Praying in tongues was the making of his life."[3]

Missionary to Hong Kong Jackie Pullinger said, "She saw little ministry success until she began to pray consistently in other tongues. Then the Spirit began to work, and no one works like Him."[4]

Mark Buntain, Assemblies of God missionary to India, seemed to always be praying in the Spirit. Could that be a key as to how he accomplished all that he did in India?

The pastor of a great church known to be built on prayer was asked, "How do you pray so much?" One of the keys he shared was, "I pray in the Spirit."

Paul said,

"I thank my God I speak with tongues more than you all" (I Corinthians 14:18 NKJV).

Mahesh Chavda in his book *The Hidden Power of Speaking in Tongues* suggests that we take a half an hour to pray in the Spirit every day.[5] Jackie Pullinger said, "Take fifteen minutes to pray in the Spirit every day."

Years ago, I didn't do that. I would pray in the Spirit when I felt like it, or I would pray in the Spirit when I had really big problems. If I had regular sized problems, I'd just pray in English. If I had really big problems, then I'd pray in the Spirit. After reading Mahesh Chavda's challenge, I was challenged to take the time to pray in the Spirit every day as part of my regular prayer time and at times throughout the day. I wasn't going to wait until I felt like it, or until I had really big problems, but every day I would set aside time to pray in the Spirit.

When I did that, things began to change in me. I found things began to change in the ministry. I think Jackie Pullinger was onto something when she said she began to pray in the Spirit and He began to work, and no one works like Him!

So what happens when we pray in the Spirit, in that unlearned language? Paul tells us,

"...pray in the Spirit on all occasions with all kinds of prayers and requests..." (Ephesians 6:18 NIV).

10 THINGS THAT HAPPEN WHEN WE PRAY IN THE HOLY SPIRIT

1. We Can Pray for Unknown Needs

If we don't pray in the Spirit, we only pray for things we know about and whatever we may know about them. That can be very limited knowledge. On the other hand, when we pray in the Spirit we can pray for things we may not know about, needs that are unknown to us.

Paul said,

"Likewise the Spirit also helps us in our weaknesses. For we do not know what we should pray for as we ought, but the Spirit Himself makes intercession for us ...." (Romans 8:26 NKJV).

I compare praying in the Spirit to being like the "smart bombs" that our fighter pilots dropped over their targets during our military campaigns in Iraq and Afghanistan. The pilots didn't see the targets, but when they dropped the bombs, they went to exactly the right place. One of the Taliban members in Afghanistan lamented that they could put a tin can outside their tent, and the pilots could hit it.

Praying in the Spirit is like dropping "spiritual smart bombs." We don't know what we are praying but those prayers pray for exactly the right thing in exactly the right way, and God hears and God answers.

Paul says,

"...He who searches the hearts knows what the mind of the Spirit is, because He makes interces-sion for the saints according to the will of God." (Romans 8:27 NKJV).

Many testimonies have been shared how people have felt prompted to pray for someone, but they didn't know what to pray for so they started to pray in their unlearned language. Later they found out what the situation was and how God had intervened. The key was people praying in the Spirit. They didn't know what they were praying, but the Holy Spirit did, and God heard, and God answered.

People have sometimes said, "But I don't know what I'm praying." You don't need to know, God knows and He's the one who answers.

2. We Can Pray for Inexpressible Needs

Have you ever hurt or grieved so bad that you couldn't even put it into words? Have you ever faced a situation so surprising that you couldn't find the words to pray? Have you ever faced a situation that was so complex, so complicated, or such a tangled mess that you had no idea how to pray for it?

In those times the baptized in the Holy Spirit believer can pray in their unlearned language. As we pray in that unlearned language, we are praying for those things we could not find the words to pray for.

Paul referred to this in Romans,

"...but the Spirit Himself makes intercession for us with groanings which cannot be uttered." (Romans 8:26 NKJV).

I remember an incident that happened to one of the families in our first pastorate. The family owned a dairy farm and one day their teenage son got his leg caught in the PTO shaft of the tractor. The PTO shaft cut through the bones, muscles, and tendons, and his foot was left just barely attached to his leg. In a state of shock, he managed to get his leg free from the PTO shaft and he climbed back on the seat of the tractor and drove it back to the house. When he arrived back at the house, he called out for help and then passed out and fell from the seat of the tractor. His mother heard the cry for help and ran outside. There she saw her teenage son lying on the ground with his leg bleeding and foot barely attached. She later said to me, "Pastor, I couldn't think of what to pray, all I could do was to begin to pray in tongues."

Meanwhile, another family member also heard the cry for help and ran outside. They saw what had happened and ran back inside and called the rescue squad. The rescue squad came and brought the injured boy to the nearest large hospital which was in Fargo, ND.

Between what God did supernaturally and the doctors did medically, they attached the foot back onto his leg. Today he walks without a limp or any evidence of the accident except for a scar on his ankle that reminds him that one day there was an accident, but God did a miracle.

What was a key to that miracle? When the mother didn't know how to pray, she prayed in the Spirit, in that unlearned language, and God heard, and God answered, and God did a miracle!

That's what can happen when we pray in the Spirit! God hears. God answers. And God still does miracles.

Over the years in our travels we have occasionally crossed paths with this teenager who was hurt in that accident and who now is a young man. He walks without a limp or any outward evidence of that accident except for the scars on his ankle.

3. We Can Intimately Worship God in Another Dimension

When we are baptized in the Holy Spirit, we obtain a whole new dimension of worship available to us. We can sing in our native language and we can also sing in our unlearned language.

Paul said,

"...I will sing with the Spirit, and I will also sing with the understanding." (I Corinthians 14:15 NKJV).

I will never forget when this dawned on me. I had already been baptized in the Holy Spirit for several years and had been pastoring for a few years. One of the things that I did each week in our first pastorate was to pick a day out of the week to visit everybody in the hospital located in town. Now you have to understand that sounds a whole lot more impressive than it really was. For you see there were only about 750 people in town and there were never more than a half a dozen people in the hospital. I would just go down the hallway and visit in any room that had a patient in it.

One afternoon as I was walking down the hallway, a voice cried out from one of the rooms, "Preacher, I'm not ready to die." As I looked into the room, there was the most well-known atheist in town. He had no time for God, no interest in God. He thought anyone who believed in and served God was a fool.

Earlier that afternoon, however; a doctor had told him he had terminal cancer with two weeks to live. It's amazing how interested in God an atheist becomes when he finds out he's going to die.

That afternoon I had the privilege of telling the town atheist about Jesus. He believed what I shared with him, and he accepted Christ. After that, he told everyone who came to his room what he had done. He told everyone he had given his life to Christ.

Two weeks later he died and his family had to make plans for his funeral. He was a bachelor and obviously he had no church that he belonged to. Half of his relatives belonged to a certain church in town and thought their pastor should do the funeral. The other half of his relatives had no church affiliation, and they thought I should do the funeral because I was the one he had called out to in the hospital and had told him about Jesus. The family argued back and forth and finally decided to have both of us pastors do the funeral.

On the day of the funeral, they were going to have a meal prior to the funeral at the home of one of the family members. As I was driving on my way to the home, I realized that I could sing in the Spirit. I started to sing in the Spirit and all the way to the home I was singing in the Spirit. I had found another way to worship God.

I was disappointed when I got to the house because I had to stop singing in the Spirit. After the meal, I got back in my car and drove to the funeral home, again singing in the Spirit all the way there. People perhaps wondered why that man's mouth was moving when no one else was in the car.

When I arrived at the funeral home the other pastor was already there, and he said, "You speak first, and I'll finish." I said, "Fine." The funeral started and after a few songs, it was my turn. I shared with them what had happened that afternoon in the hospital. How I was going down the hospital hallway when a voice called out from one of the rooms, "Preacher, I'm not ready to die". I shared how I went into the room and told him about Jesus, and he believed what I shared with him and gave his life to Christ. Because of that, today he is in heaven. I then shared a few other things and sat down in chair, out of sight, off to the side.

It was now the other pastor's turn, but he had a theological issue to deal with. His church didn't believe anyone was saved unless they laid hands on them and they remitted their sins. He had a choice to either try to discredit me and everything I had said or stay true to his erroneous doctrine. He chose to try to discredit me and everything I had said. It was not a pretty afternoon. In fact, it was so bad that the people of his church came up to me after the funeral and asked me if I was all right.

Meanwhile, while he was trying to discredit me and everything I had said, there was only one thing going through my mind. "I can't wait to get in the car and sing in the Spirit again." I had found an additional way to worship God.

4. We Can Build Ourselves Up Spiritually

As we pray in the Spirit, we build ourselves up spiritually.

Jude said,

"...beloved, building yourselves up on your most holy faith, praying in the Holy Spirit," (Jude 20 NKJV).

When we pray in the Holy Spirit, in our unlearned language, we build ourselves up spiritually. We are "recharging our spiritual batteries."

In the March 2008 edition of *Charisma Magazine* there was an article about Missionary Jackie Pullinger. She said that after she was baptized in the Holy Spirit, she didn't use it at first. About a year later she met a couple who told her, "The scripture says if you pray in tongues you will be built up spiritually. It doesn't say you will feel built up". After that, she started to pray in the Spirit, and it changed her life and ministry.[6]

5. We Can Become More Spiritually Sensitive

Remember the old radios that had a dial you had to turn to tune in the station you wanted? You had to turn the dial to just the right place in order for the station to come in clearly.

I compare praying in our unlearned language to being like turning that radio dial to just the right place so we can hear the station clearly. When we pray in our unlearned language, it makes us sensitive to the Holy Spirit so we can hear the voice of the Holy Spirit clearly.

It also can be pictured like putting up an antenna higher so you can receive a radio or television signal more clearly.

Jackie Pullinger said that after she had begun to pray in tongues, people started coming to Christ in her ministry. At first, she thought that perhaps it was because her Chinese had improved. Then she realized that her Chinese was no better than it had been before.[7]

The only change was that she had begun to pray in the Spirit, and she then found herself at the right place, at the right time saying the right thing to the right people. After being baptized in the Holy Spirit, she realized that being effective in the work of the Kingdom was not as much a matter of skill, or of education, as being sensitive to what God is saying and doing than anything else.

One time Jackie had been trying to bring an old Chinese woman who had been a life-long follower of Buddha to Christ. Jackie was seemingly making no progress so she decided to pray in the Spirit for the lady. One day as she was praying in the Spirit for her, the word "vegetable" came to her. She went to the lady's son and asked, "Would the word 'vegetable' mean anything to your mother?" He said, "Oh yes, all her life my mother has only eaten vegetables in order to please her god." With that revelation, Jackie went to the old Buddhist woman and said to her, "I want you to know that God so loves you for trying all your life to please him by only eating vegetables, and He has sent me here today to introduce you to Him, His name is Jesus." With that revelation of "vegetables," she led that life-long Buddhist to Jesus.[8]

What was the key to that testimony? It was the revelation of the word "vegetables." Where did that information come from? When she didn't know how to reach that old Buddhist woman she prayed in the Spirit and the Holy Spirit revealed the key to her.

The baptism in the Holy Spirit allows us to pray in the Holy Spirit, which sharpens and fine tunes our ability to hear the things that need to be heard in order to effectively minister.

Jackie Pullinger said that as she began using her unlearned language, it opened new doors. She said, "I would walk down the street, bump into a gangster—some of them I knew, some of them I didn't—and they all started to believe in Jesus, and I saw people healed... Because I was praying in the Holy Spirit, God was able to lead me to people He had gotten ready."[9]

6. We Can Sense the Presence of God

When we pray in our unlearned language, we can sense the presence of God.

7. We Can Bypass the Mind

Often our natural mind can mess up our praying. Our prayers can become very self-centered and self-serving. Jackie Pullinger said, "The problem is, most of us have got an agenda, and we say, 'This is what I want to do, dear Lord, please bless me'...But when you pray in tongues it's the opposite way around. It's. 'Dear Lord, You've got an agenda, and I'd like to play the part You want me to play in it.'"[10]

When we pray in our unlearned language, we tap into God's agenda rather than trying to get God to "buy" into our agenda.

Science confirms that when we pray in the Spirit, we bypass the mind. Research done at the University of Pennsylvania on speaking in tongues found that the frontal lobes — the thinking, willful part of the brain through which people control what they do — were relatively quiet, as were the language centers. Since the human language center of the brain is quiet, science supports the fact that genuine tongues come from outside the believer. They further reported that the person receives positive effects, pleasure, and positive emotions. Science affirms that tongues come from outside the mind of the believer.[11] The Holy Spirit is talking through them bypassing the mind.

8. We Can Experience Inner Healing

When we pray in our unlearned language, it can bring inner healing. I remember hearing Dr. Richard Dobbins, a counselor, psychologist, and founder of Emerge Ministries; say at a conference that being baptized in the Holy Spirit and speaking in tongues is not a mental health problem but has tremendous mental health benefits.

I heard a minister share how as a young man he had given his life to Christ. Later he ended up in the military and in the front lines of battle. There in the front lines of battle, he saw things that were horrible to see and experienced horrifying things. He served his tour of duty honorably, and when his tour of duty was completed, he came home with an honorable discharge. He also came home with nightmares that caused him to wake up screaming in the night. He tried various things to stop the nightmares, but nothing worked.

One Sunday night he was walking down the street in one of our cities in America, and he noticed a church service in progress. It was an Assemblies of God church, and he decided to go in. He had never been to an Assemblies of God service before. That night the preacher spoke on the baptism in the Holy Spirit and at the end of the service when the altar call was given for those who wanted to receive the baptism in the Holy Spirit he went forward. That night as he was prayed for, he received the baptism in the Holy Spirit.

He said that night he went home and slept the entire night. He said from that night on he never had another military nightmare. What happened? The Holy Spirit brought healing deep down inside where only the Holy Spirit can bring healing when we give Him total access to our life.

Another example of inner healing is a testimony I read in Dr. Wade Goodall's book *The Blessing*. Doctor Goodall shared the story of a young couple whose wedding he performed. The marriage started out great but as time went on it began to deteriorate. It got to the point where Dr. Goodall thought their marriage was another divorce statistic just waiting to happen. Because this couple lived in another country, some time passed before Dr. Goodall heard from them again. When the young man called, he was so excited. He said, "Things have never been better. Our family has never been better. I love my wife and children more than ever." Doctor Goodall was thrilled but puzzled and asked the young husband and father, "What happened?" The young man said, "Things got so bad I couldn't pray in English anymore. He said I just started to pray in tongues and God began to change me. He said over a period of time I began to love my wife more. I began to love my children more." What happened? God did a healing deep down inside of him and changed him and the marriage was restored.[12]

In a letter sent to all the ministers of our District, one of the counselors from our District said, "Take time to pray in the Spirit every day."

As Dr. Dobbins said, "It's not a mental health problem, but has tremendous mental health benefits."

In fact, a recent study done in England found that those who engaged in the practice of speaking in tongues were more emotionally stable than those who did not. [13]

9. We Can Experience a Clearing and Settling of Our Mind

Have you ever noticed how at times our mind will seemingly go like a pinball in a pinball machine? It bounces all over the place.

Beth and I were at a writer's conference where we were told that the best thing you can do before you begin to write is to pray in the Spirit. It clears and settles the mind which then, in turn, helps us to focus, to think clearly and to hear what the Holy Spirit is saying.

One preacher told of how when he was first baptized in the Holy Spirit it would bother him when he was praying in the Spirit and all these earthly things would come to his mind. Soon he realized that it was God giving him solutions to problems he was facing. God was giving him answers to questions he was asking. He said he learned to have paper and pencil with him, and he would write down what God was saying and then go back to praying.

The key was that as he prayed in the Spirit, it cleared and settled his mind so he could hear what the Spirit was saying.

Some years ago we had people stopping at our product table before and after the services asking if we accepted credit cards. At that time we only accepted checks or cash. After being asked about credit cards by numerous people, we decided to get set up to accept credit cards. I went to our local bank and asked if we could get set up to accept credit cards through them. They said we could, so we filled out all the paperwork, turned it in and waited. We waited for weeks, perhaps even months. When we would check on the progress, they couldn't understand what the holdup was.

One day after I had been praying in the Spirit the thought came to my mind to go check with our local credit union to see if they could set us up to accept credit cards. Later that day I went to the credit union, told them what we wanted to do, and they had us set up to accept credit cards within a couple of days.

I'm convinced that the Holy Spirit gave me that directive and by praying in the Spirit, it cleared and settled my mind so I could hear what the Holy Spirit had to say.

10. We Can Drink of the Rivers of Living Water

When we pray in the Spirit, it brings refreshing. We drink of the rivers of living water Jesus spoke of. It quenches the spiritual thirst in our lives.

It is said that someone approached Smith Wigglesworth, the well-known evangelist who had a powerful ministry years ago, and said, "Brother Wigglesworth, don't you ever take a vacation?" "Every day," he responded. "What do you mean?" they asked. He responded, "I pray in tongues daily, and I get refreshed. That's my vacation, that's my holiday."[14]

Of course, we need to have a time of vacation and a time of rest. The Bible tells us Jesus told His disciple to "come apart and rest." The Bible speaks of having a Sabbath. We need to take the time to rest and have vacations.

But let's not miss the truth of what Smith Wigglesworth was saying. When we pray in the Spirit, it brings refreshing and renewal to our lives. It's like having a short rest, a mini-vacation every day.

Jesus said,

"...out of his heart will flow rivers of living water" (John 7:38 NKJV).

SUMMARY

We could summarize everything that has been said in this chapter by saying that as we pray in the Spirit, in our unlearned language, we release the Holy Spirit to work. Doctor George Wood said that as we pray in the Spirit, it catapults our experience beyond the natural into the supernatural.[15]

The enemy, the devil, knows how powerful this weapon is, and he will try everything to get the Spirit-filled believer to not put this powerful weapon to use. He will try to convince you that it's a waste of time, God doesn't hear you, God can't understand you, you're making it all up, and many other lies. Don't let him deceive you! He's a liar!

If we put to use this simple truth and take the time to pray in the Spirit each day, we will find ourselves saying as Jackie Pullinger did, "I started to pray in the Spirit and then He began to work, and no one works like Him."

Over the years as we have preached on this subject, we've had people come back to us and tell us when they began to pray in the Spirit it changed things in their lives, in their ministries, at their places of employment, etc.

Let's put to fullest use what we have received. To not put the baptism in the Holy Spirit to use by praying in the Spirit would be like getting a wonderful gift for Christmas and then letting it sit in a closet. Let's be people who consistently take time to pray in the Spirit.

REVIEW AND DISCUSSION QUESTIONS

1. What did Paul mean when he said, "be filled with the Spirit"?

2. Why do so many people who have been baptized in the Holy Spirit not pray in the Spirit regularly?

3. Why pray in the Spirit? What happens when we pray in the Spirit?

4. What lies will the enemy use to discourage people from praying in the Spirit?

5. Why does the enemy try so hard to prevent people from praying in the Spirit?

Chapter Eight

PENTECOSTAL EXPLOSION

There is an explosion taking place in the church today! Not in three weeks! Not in three months! Not in three years! But today! Let me illustrate.

It seems like all you hear today is how much Islam is growing around the world today and how many Muslims there are today. Statistics tell us that there are 1.3 billion Muslims in the world today.[1] But did you know that there are 2.3 billion Christians in the world today?[2] There are one billion more followers of Christ than there are followers of Mohammed in the world today.

And yes, Islam is growing. But do you know that Christianity is the fastest growing religion? More new Christians are added than any other religion.[3]

Figures tell us that every day 32,000 people in Africa give their life to Christ. Every day 25,000 people in Asia give their life to Christ. Every day 17,000 people in Latin America give their life to Christ.[4]

When you add what God is doing in Africa, to what God is doing in Asia, to what God is doing in Latin America to what God is doing in the rest of the world; every day 82,000 people give their life to Christ.[5] Every day!

There is an explosion happening in the church world today, and it's a Pentecostal explosion. The Pentecostal part of the church world is not in the background watching what God is doing around the world, but instead is at the very cutting edge of what God is doing around the world. Most of what is happening in the church world today is happening in the Pentecostal part of the church world.

Today there are over 650 million baptized in the Holy Spirit believers in the world right now.[6] Do you realize how many people that is? That's approximately two times the entire United States population! That's a lot of people baptized in the Holy Spirit and every day that number increases. Statistics tell us that every day 27,000 people are baptized in the Holy Spirit around the world.[7]

Pew Forum on Religion and Public Life did a survey that was published in *Today's Pentecostal Evangel*. The survey showed that Pentecostals and Charismatics together comprise at least one half the population of Brazil. At least one half the population of Guatemala. At least one half the population of Kenya. At least 44 percent of the Philippines. About one-third of the population of South Africa. About one-third the population of Chile. About one-fourth the population of Nigeria. About one-fourth of the United States. About 11 percent of South Korea. The survey revealed how powerfully the Holy Spirit is moving around the world. There is an explosion happening in the church world today, and it's a Pentecostal explosion.[8]

One example is what happened in Malawi, Africa. The General Superintendent of the Assemblies of God in Malawi, Lazarus Chakwara, was asked how the Malawi Assemblies of God had grown from 165 churches to nearly 3,000 churches and preaching points in a fifteen-year period. His response was, "God dealt with us about preaching Pentecost. At first, we set a goal of having three-fifths of our believers filled with the Spirit. We decided that wasn't scriptural, so we changed our strategy and preached that everyone should be filled with the Holy Spirit according to Acts 2:4..."[9] The result was a spiritual explosion in Malawi.

Life magazine has called the Pentecostal Movement one of the greatest events of the last century![10]

The key to the Pentecostal explosion happening around the world today is the baptism in the Holy Spirit.

What God said in Zechariah is still true today.

"...Not by might nor by power, but by My Spirit..." (Zechariah 4:6 NKJV).

God has never printed a retraction. God has never printed a correction. Therefore it's still true today. It's not by our might, nor by our power, but by His Spirit. It was the secret back then, and it's still the secret today. It's the secret for life, for ministry and for the church.

PETER'S SECRET

What Peter could not accomplish by might and power, he did through the Holy Spirit. For three and a half years Peter followed Jesus. Where Jesus went, Peter went. What Jesus said, Peter heard. What Jesus did, Peter saw. For three and a half years, Peter followed Jesus but on the night when Jesus was arrested, Peter denied Him three times before servant girls. Paraphrasing Peter's response, Peter said, "I don't know Him! I never met Him! I don't have anything to do with Him!"

Fifty days later we find this same Peter publicly and powerfully preaching before thousands. What had happened to Him? He had received the baptism in the Holy Spirit! Now, he was publicly and powerfully preaching before thousands.

What conclusion we can draw? The baptism in the Holy Spirit accomplished in his life what walking side by side with Jesus for three and a half years could not.

EARLY CHURCH'S SECRET

What was the secret of the Early Church? Think with me for a moment about the Day of Pentecost and the 120 who were gathered together in that upper room.

First, let's look at the room. The room was borrowed. It was rented. They didn't even own the room!

Second, the room was very small according to our standards today. According to an article I recall reading, some researchers and historians believe that the upper room was possibly only 400 square feet in size. It was 20 feet by 20 feet, about the size of a two-car garage!

Then let's look at the people. There were 120 there on the Day of Pentecost. You might say, "Well that's not a bad sized group." But did you ever wonder where the rest of them were? On one occasion alone, after His resurrection, Jesus appeared to five hundred. Paul mentions this in his letter to the Corinthians in I Corinthians 15:6. Undoubtedly they would have gotten the message that they were to wait in Jerusalem for the baptism in the Holy Spirit. So of this one group alone, most of them were missing. There were only 120 in the Upper Room. That's less than 25% of just that one group. Where were the rest of them? Perhaps they didn't think this was important. Maybe they were too busy. Perhaps they had other things to do. Maybe they couldn't fit in the room. Regardless of the reason, there were only 120 in the Upper Room, but those 120 went out and turned their world upside down.

What was their secret? The secret wasn't the room. It was borrowed and very small. It wasn't the number of people. Most of them were missing. The secret was what happened in that room. They received the baptism in the Holy Spirit. The secret was that they left that room with the baptism in the Holy Spirit! They went out proclaiming the gospel and turned their world upside down.

Some would say, that can't be. It must have been the size of their churches. That's how they turned their world upside down. Pentecost was the birth of the church so prior to this they didn't even have any churches. Once churches were established the average size of the average local church in the Early Church era was about sixty people. Their secret wasn't the size of their churches.

Well, then it must have been the wonderful culture they were in. No, that wasn't it either. We have to remember they did not live in a Judeo-Christian culture. They lived in a pre-Christian culture. A culture that often was hostile to Christianity. They didn't have equal rights laws nor did they have anti-discrimination laws in their culture. Often when people came to Christ, they lost their jobs. If they owned a business, people would stop doing business with them. The culture they lived in was not a Judeo-Christian culture. That wasn't their secret.

Then the government must have been the reason multitudes were coming to Christ. No, the government was often very anti-Christian. For example, Nero was the Roman emperor during part of this time. He would tie Christians to posts in his garden and say, "You people say you are the light of the world then light up my world," and he would burn them to death. Also, during this period the Romans would sew Christians up inside animal skins and then toss them into the arena for a lion or tiger to tear apart. This was considered sport. The government wasn't their secret either.

Their secret wasn't the room; it was borrowed and pitifully small. It wasn't the number of people. It wasn't the size of their churches. It wasn't the culture they were in. It wasn't the government. Their secret was the power of the baptism in the Holy Spirit. It was the secret back then, and it's still the secret today!

THE SECRET TODAY

The secret today isn't the room you have. The secret isn't the number of people you have. The secret isn't the size of your church. The secret isn't the culture we live in. The secret isn't the government. The secret is the power of the Holy Spirit. It was the secret back then, and it's still the secret today.

People sometimes say God can't work where we are because we don't have our own building. Or we don't have enough people. Or our church isn't big enough. Or we live in a post-Christian era. Or a certain political party is in office.

Having our own building is nice. It's nice to have numbers. It's nice to have a big building. It would be nice to be in a Christian culture. And it would be nice to have a Christian government. But, these are not requirements. These are not the secret. The secret is the power of the Holy Spirit.

Through the power of the Holy Spirit, Jesus can build his church any place and anywhere. Seeing Jesus build his church is not dependent on your building, your numbers, the culture or the government. It's dependent on the power and working of the Holy Spirit.

Beth and I were at a mission's convention in Iowa, raising support to go minister on the Holy Spirit in the country of East Timor. Also, at that mission's convention was a missionary to China. I asked her how many believers in China were baptized in the Holy Spirit. Without hesitation, she said, "About ninety-percent." No wonder thousands are coming to Christ every day in China. People come to Christ. Then they are told about the baptism in the Holy Spirit and they get baptized in the Holy Spirit. They then go out in the power of the Holy Spirit and reach their friends for Christ and the cycle is repeated again and again.

Today we find many models for the church in the church world. But I think it was Jack Hayford who summarized it best when he said, "It won't be our model that penetrates our society but the power of the Holy Spirit." That was the secret of the Early Church.

PENTECOSTAL CHALLENGE

When you buy a new piece of electronic equipment; a cell phone, a camera, or a computer, you get an operation manual. It tells you how to make it work, and what you need to make it work.

Our operations manual, the Bible, tells us we need the baptism in the Holy Spirit. Not in order to be saved. We are saved through a commitment of our life to Christ. Nothing else! Nothing more! But in order to be all that Jesus wants us to be and to do all that Jesus wants us to do we need the baptism in the Holy Spirit.

Without the baptism in the Holy Spirit, we cannot be the people of the book of Acts. Without the baptism in the Holy Spirit, we cannot do what the people of the book of Acts did. We need to have what they had in order to be what they were and to do what they did.

I believe the closer we get to Jesus' return the more important baptism in the Holy Spirit will become. Compared to other nations we have it so easy in America today, but there are storm clouds on the horizon.

Things could change economically in America. There are storm clouds on the horizon; the escalating astronomic national debt, the volatility of the stock market, the uncertainty of gas prices, etc.

Things could change socially in America. There are storm clouds on the horizon. The decisions electorates are making. The decisions courts are making. The decisions judges are making, etc.

In times of change, the baptism in the Holy Spirit becomes even more important. The baptism in the Holy Spirit will help us to stand strong, to be what Jesus wants us to be and to do what Jesus wants us to do.

All through church history, the church has always been at its best when things have been their worst in the world. An example would be what happened during the period known as the Great Depression. It was during this period that the number of Assemblies of God churches tripled. The number of people in Assemblies of God churches almost tripled. It was also during this period that four of our Bible Colleges started. It was one of the greatest periods in Assemblies of God history. What was the secret? The power of the baptism in the Holy Spirit.

SUMMARY

The secret today is still,

"...not by might nor by power, but by My Spirit says the Lord..." (Zechariah 4:6 NKJV).

We need to be like the Early Church, full of the Holy Spirit and fresh in the Holy Spirit, and I'm convinced that our greatest days are still ahead.

REVIEW AND DISCUSSION QUESTIONS

1. What is the secret to what God is doing in the Pentecostal part of the church world? Why is the Pentecostal part of the church world exploding in growth?

2. What was Peter's secret to his incredible transformation from someone who could not stand for Christ before servant girls to someone who was publicly and powerfully preaching before thousands?

3. What was the secret to what the Early Church was able to accomplish?

4. Is Jesus' ability to build His church dependent on the size of your building, the size of your church, the post-Christian culture we are in, or the political party in office?

5. Why will the baptism in the Holy Spirit become even more important as we get closer to the return of Christ?

Chapter Nine

PREVENTING A POWERLESS PENTECOST

The story is told about some folks who were new to boating. They had bought a new 22-foot boat and decided to take it for a ride on the lake. Unfortunately, the boat was extremely sluggish. Finally, they decided to go back to port to get help at the local marina. A good topside check revealed everything was in good working order so the marina sent a diver down to check the underside of the boat. A few moments later the diver came up laughing. Under the boat, securely still strapped in place was the trailer!

Sometimes things don't work the way they're supposed to because of the things we do. This same thing can happen regarding the baptism in the Holy Spirit.

The title of this chapter would appear to be an oxymoron, a contradiction in terms, an impossibility. How can you have a powerless Pentecost? How can you have a powerless baptism in the Holy Spirit? How can you have a powerless baptized-in-the-Holy-Spirit believer?

After all, didn't Jesus say in Acts 1:8,

"... you shall receive power when the Holy Spirit has come upon you ... " (NKJV).

So how can a powerless Pentecost be possible?

POWER OF PENTECOST

The Greek word that is translated "power" in Acts 1:8 is "dunamis." We get our word "dynamo" from this same root word. The Greek word literally means "ability" and "enablement."

We can find the power of Pentecost illustrated in several ways.

Look at Scripture

We find that after the promise of the baptism in the Holy Spirit and power was fulfilled in Acts 2, the early disciples went out in power. The same disciples, who on the night Jesus was arrested, had hidden, scattered, and fled; later went out with power. They went out boldly, standing for Christ, witnessing for Christ and ministering for Christ. It didn't matter what was done to them. It didn't matter what they were threatened with. It didn't matter where they were. They went out in power!

If they were threatened with whipping, their attitude was "go ahead, we've been through it before." If they were threatened with prison, their attitude was, "go ahead, we've been there before." If they were threatened with death, their attitude was, "go ahead, to be absent from the body is to be present with the Lord" (II Corinthians 5:8).

They went out in power. It can't be denied! Scripture records it. All we have to do is look at scripture.

Look at History

As we look at history, we find the power of Pentecost illustrated. I heard a message in which the speaker quoted facts and figures that were compiled by Vinson Synan, a well-known and respected researcher. The figures are concrete, undeniable facts from history.

In 1907 the Church of God in Christ divided over the issue of the baptism in the Holy Spirit and speaking in tongues. One group followed Charles Mason. The other group followed C.P. Jones. By 1964, C.P. Jones' group, the group that didn't believe in the baptism in the Holy Spirit, had 146 churches and 7,621 people. Charles Mason's group, the group that believed in the baptism in the Holy Spirit, had 4,000 churches and 400,000 people. They had 27 times more churches and 52 times more people. What was the difference? The baptism in the Holy Spirit.[1]

In 1901 the Methodist church in Chile divided over the issue of the baptism in the Holy Spirit. At that time there were 6,000 Methodists in Chile. By 1986, the group that did not believe in the baptism in the Holy Spirit had 5,000 members. The group that believed in the baptism in the Holy Spirit had almost 2,000,000 members. What was the difference? The baptism in the Holy Spirit.[2]

These are just two examples. All we have to do is look at history to see the power of Pentecost illustrated.

Look at Today

As we look at what is happening today, we again see the power of Pentecost illustrated. As we mentioned earlier, there are over 650 million baptized in the Holy Spirit believers today.[3] Everyday 27,000 people are baptized in the Holy Spirit.[4] I read recently where 80-90% of all Protestant church growth since 1950 has been Pentecostal. I also read where 27.7% of all Christians are baptized in the Holy Spirit today. That's up from .005% in 1900.[5]

The PE News reported that the Assemblies of God in 2015 had 67,992,330 adherents in more than 365,000 churches throughout the world. That's a staggering 72.7 percent growth in worldwide adherents since 1989.[6]

All we have to do is look at what is happening today, and we see the power of Pentecost illustrated.

The power of Pentecost. It's undeniable! All we have to do is:

- look at scripture
- look at history
- look at today

POWERLESS PENTECOST

In light of all we have said about the power of Pentecost and looking at scripture, history and what is happening today; you can find people today with a powerless Pentecost. They received the baptism in the Holy Spirit but today find themselves weak and powerless.

One reason is that people sometimes have a misconception and misunderstanding regarding the baptism in the Holy Spirit. They think that if they are baptized in the Holy Spirit, they can neglect or violate other areas of their Christian life and still have the power of Pentecost flowing in their lives. In reality, violating or neglecting in these areas will short-circuit the power of the baptism in the Holy Spirit.

Let me illustrate it this way. You can have a fully-functioning electrical power source and a fully-functional light, but if you have a short-circuit in the wiring, the light will not work. It doesn't matter how powerful the power source is, it doesn't matter how many promises have been made about what the power can do in the light; if you have a short in the wiring, it won't work. Some would quickly blame the power source, but that's not the problem. The problem is a short in the wiring.

In the same way, we can short-circuit the power of the baptism in the Holy Spirit. The problem is not with the baptism in the Holy Spirit. The problem is the short-circuit in the spiritual wiring of our life. That's how we can end up with a powerless Pentecost.

PREVENTING A POWERLESS PENTECOST

So what can short-circuit the power and working of the baptism in the Holy Spirit in someone's life? Let me mention eight potential causes.

The Short-Circuit of Unforgiveness

Unforgiveness will short-circuit the power of the baptism in the Holy Spirit. Bitterness, animosity, and division will all short circuit the power of the baptism in the Holy Spirit and lead to a powerless Pentecost.

At times we all will get hurt by family, friends, strangers, and even others in the church. We all have been, and we all will be hurt from time to time. Yes, even in the church.

I heard Brian Huston, pastor of Hillsong Church in Australia, give this great insight. Do you know how to get hurt in church? Just stay long enough. If you stay long enough anywhere, someone will say something you didn't like or do something you didn't like. Or, they won't say something you wanted them to say or they won't do something you wanted them to do. It will happen anywhere if you stay long enough.

The best thing to do is "get over it!" Forgive them. Unforgiveness is not worth hanging on to it because it short-circuits the power of the Holy Spirit. It's just not worth it!

The Short-Circuit of Unsubmissiveness

Not being submissive to the authorities in our life will short-circuit the power of the baptism in the Holy Spirit in our life. We all have authorities in our life. God is the ultimate authority in our life. The government is another authority in our life. Our boss at work is an authority in our life. Our spiritual leaders are authorities in our life. For a young people still living at home, their parents are authorities in their life. We all have authorities in our life.

A person cannot live in rebellion to the authorities in their life and in the power of the Holy Spirit at the same time. Rebellion will short-circuit the power of the baptism in the Holy Spirit.

One day after returning from a ministry trip, when I checked our voice mails there was a message from a very angry man. I'm not sure why he had called us because he wasn't angry with us. Perhaps he just needed someone to vent to, and he had picked up one of our prayer cards somewhere where we had ministered. The gist of his message was, "no man is going to tell me what to do, I answer only to God!" This man was irate and angry with his pastor. He had a submission problem, and until he rectified his submission problem, he would not experience the power of the Holy Spirit as he could.

Of course, if those in authority are asking us to do something contrary to scripture, then we are to obey God rather than men. For example, before going into the ministry, I worked in retail management. One day my boss, the General Manager, asked me to deliberately break some merchandise so we would have enough broken merchandise to file a claim with the trucking company. What had broken in shipment wasn't enough to meet the minimum requirements to file a claim. I said, "I can't do that. That's not right." Another example was when a trucking company would accidently bring in a box of merchandise intended for another store into our store. The boss wanted me to keep the merchandise and put our price tag on it and sell it. He justified it by saying, people steal from us and we're just getting even. Again I had to say, "No, that's not right, I won't do it." So in these kinds of cases, when asked by our authorities to do what is wrong according to scripture we are to do what is right rather than submit. In all other cases, we are to submit to the authorities in our life.

The late Adrian Rogers, a great Baptist pastor said, "We will never be over the things God wants us to be over until we are under the things God wants us to be under."

The Short-Circuit of Not Being Loving

Acting unlovingly will short-circuit the power of the baptism in the Holy Spirit. While the baptism in the Holy Spirit is a "baptism in love," as the late David Wilkerson called it, we must reach out in love. As we reach out in love, the baptism in the Holy Spirit will give us the ability, the enablement to love.

On the other hand, we cannot act unlovingly toward our spouse, our leaders, our co-workers, or our neighbors and still experience the power of the Holy Spirit. The lack of reaching out in love will short-circuit the power of the baptism in the Holy Spirit.

The Short-Circuit of Self-Centeredness

If our lives revolve around self, we will short-circuit the power of the baptism in the Holy Spirit. The power is given for a purpose, to serve Christ and His Kingdom. Self-centered people will not experience the power of the baptism in the Holy Spirit.

On a radio broadcast, I heard a minister make the observation that 80% of believers in America have never submitted to the Lordship of Christ. What he was saying was that they have asked Jesus to be their Savior but have not made Him their Lord. To them, the Christian life is all about them. Christ is just a means of serving themselves. He's just an addition to their life of living for themselves, a means of "self-enhancement." Using Christ rather than serving Christ.

With that mindset, they will never experience the power of the baptism in the Holy Spirit as they could.

Paul said,

"If then you were raised with Christ, seek those things which are above...Set your mind on things above, not on things on the earth." (Colossians 3:1-2 NKJV).

Christ is to be the focus of our life.

Paul said,

"...Christ who is our life..." (Colossians 3:4 NKJV).

"...to live is Christ..." (Philippians 1:21 NKJV).

Christ was his life, the focus of his life and the purpose of his life.

Self-centered believers will not experience the power of the Holy Spirit.

The Short-Circuit of Not Spending Time with God

If we don't spend time with God, we will not experience the power of the baptism in the Holy Spirit.

Look at the example of the Early Church. In Acts 2 they were baptized in the Holy Spirit. As you read through the Book of Acts, you find that they spent time with God. They prayed. They were in the Word. They worshipped. They spent time with God!

Not spending time with God will short-circuit the power of the Holy Spirit.

The Short-Circuit of Not Keeping the Baptism in the Holy Spirit Fresh

Something experienced years ago but isn't fresh in our lives today doesn't provide power for us today. As we mentioned previously, "you can't sail on yesterday's wind." You need a fresh wind today in order to sail a boat today.

We can't experience the power of the baptism in the Holy Spirit today by relying on historical infilling. We need a fresh infilling of the Holy Spirit every day. We need to pray in the Spirit every day!

That's why Paul told the believers in Ephesus,

"...be filled with the Spirit." (Ephesians 5:18 NKJV).

The Greek word that is translated "filled" literally means "keep on being filled." Paul realized, "you can't sail on yesterday's wind." You and I cannot be empowered today on a historical infilling. We need a fresh infilling every day!

I compare the baptism in the Holy Spirit to being like the manna in the Old Testament. They needed to gather the manna fresh every day. You and I need a fresh infilling of the Holy Spirit every day.

Not keeping the baptism in the Holy Spirit fresh will short-circuit the power of the baptism in the Holy Spirit.

The Short-Circuit of Sin

Unconfessed and unrepented sin in our lives will short-circuit the power of the baptism in the Holy Spirit. We can't live in sin and experience the power of the baptism in the Holy Spirit.

We need to confess our sin and ask for forgiveness. We need to repent of sin. To repent means "to turn around." We need to turn from our sin. Let's not excuse it. Let's not ignore it. Let's not make provision for it. Let's ask forgiveness for it and repent of it and experience the power of Pentecost.

The Short-Circuit of Giving in to Fear

The power of the baptism in the Holy Spirit is experienced when we step out in faith. It's like the illustration we used earlier in which electrical power in an outlet is released when you plug something into the outlet. The power is already there waiting to be released. When we are baptized in the Holy Spirit, the power enters us. Jesus said in Acts 1:8, "...you shall receive power when the Holy Spirit has come upon you..." The power is in the baptized Holy Spirit believer, but the power has to be released.

How is the power released? When we step out in faith and do what the Lord is prompting us to do. People sometimes mistakenly think they haven't received any power because they still have fears, butterflies, and apprehensions. You have the power, but you need to step out in faith, and as you do you will find the Holy Spirit will empower and enable you to rise above fear and do what God is asking you to do.

Boldness and power are not the absence of fear. They are going on in spite of it. If we wait until we have no fear and no butterflies, we will miss experiencing the unleashing of the power of the baptism in the Holy Spirit and what God could have done through us. We need to step out in spite of our fears to experience the power of the Holy Spirit.

If we give in to fear and don't step out in spite of the fear, we will short-circuit the power of the baptism in the Holy Spirit.

SUMMARY

Pentecost is powerful! The baptism in the Holy Spirit is everything Jesus said it would be. All we have to do is:

- look at scripture
- look at history
- look at today

But it's possible to have a powerless Pentecost. To short-circuit what the baptism in the Holy Spirit can do:

- by unforgiveness
- by unsubmissiveness
- by acting unlovingly
- by being self-centered
- by failing to spend time with God
- by failing to keep the baptism in the Holy Spirit fresh
- by having unconfessed, unrepented sin in our life
- by giving in to fear

Let's be people who are not going to short-circuit the power of the baptism in the Holy Spirit. We're going to:

- forgive
- be submissive to the authorities in our life
- reach out in love
- make Christ the center of our life
- spend time with God
- keep the baptism in the Holy Spirit fresh
- repent and ask forgiveness of sin in our life
- not give in to fear but instead step out in faith

REVIEW AND DISCUSSION QUESTIONS

1. In what ways do we see the power of Pentecost illustrated?

2. How is a powerless Pentecost possible? Explain the light illustration.

3. What are the potential short circuits of the power of the baptism in the Holy Spirit?

4. Take time to briefly discuss each potential short-circuit.

5. What is the opposite of each potential short-circuit?

Chapter Ten

KEEPING THE FIRE GOING

One of the things Beth and I love to do for a vacation is to go camping and fishing. I know for some that is not your idea of a vacation, but we find it very relaxing and enjoyable. To add an extra challenge to the camping experience, we try to light the first campfire with one match and keep the fire going all week long, never using another match. In order to keep the fire going we have to keep in mind the three basic requirements; (1) you need to remove the hindrances, (2) you need to have combustible material and (3) you need to have oxygen. If you don't have these three things in place, the fire will die.

One of the characteristics we see in the Early Church after they received the baptism in the Holy Spirit was their passion for God. They were on fire. How did they keep the fire going? How do we keep the spiritual fire going?

The same three basic requirements to keeping a natural fire going are required to keep the spiritual fire going in our life. We need to remove the spiritual hindrances. We need to have spiritually combustible material. We need to have spiritual oxygen. If we don't have these three things in place, the fire will not keep burning or at least not at a high level.

GOD WANTS US TO BE ON FIRE FOR HIM

Paul, in his letter to the believers in Rome, encouraged them to be "fervent in spirit" (Romans 12:11). The word translated "fervent" comes from a Greek word meaning "hot" or "boiling." The NIV translation of Romans 12:11 says,

"Never be lacking in zeal, but keep your spiritual fervor serving the Lord."

God wants us to be fervent, passionate, zealous, and on fire. He doesn't want us to be casual, apathetic, lukewarm or indifferent.

Jesus said,

"I came to send fire on the earth, and how I wish it were already kindled." (Luke 12:49 NKJV).

Paul said,

"...fan into flame the gift of God, which is in you..." (II Timothy 1:6 NIV).

"Do not put out the Spirit's fire" (I Thessalonians 5:19 NIV).

Everyone has a fire burning in the "furnace of their life" for something. Some people are on fire about sports. Others about recreation. Some about their job. Others about their hobby. Everyone has a fire burning in their life about something, but God wants us to be on fire for Him.

So, what does that mean? It means that God wants to be the most important and most exciting thing in our life. He wants to be the passion of our life!

Being on fire for God doesn't necessarily refer to how loud we are or even how demonstrative we are. It refers to God being the most important and most exciting thing in our life.

There is nothing wrong with sports, hobbies, recreation, etc. in themselves; but they were never meant to be the most important and most exciting things in our life.

God wants to be the most important, most exciting thing in our life. He wants us to be on fire for Him! Passionate about Him! And He wants us to stay on fire for Him. He has no desire for us to be "shooting stars."

Have you ever been with someone late at night and seen a shooting star? When you see it, you tell the person you are with to look, and when they look, it's gone. It was briefly on fire, but then the fire disappears. God doesn't want us to be "shooting stars." He wants us to stay on fire.

So, how do we keep the spiritual fire going? How do we keep the spiritual fire of the baptism in the Holy Spirit going in our life?

Just like keeping a fire going in the natural realm, we need to....

REMOVE THE HINDRANCES

At the campsite, if we're going to keep the fire going, we need to remove the hindrances. We need to remove any wet wood, any water, and any other hindrances from the fire ring. If we don't remove the hindrances the fire will smolder, sputter, and die.

So it is in our spiritual lives. We must remove the hindrances in order to keep the fire going.

So, what are some of the hindrances to keeping the spiritual fire going?

The Hindrance of Sin

Sin is a hindrance to keeping the spiritual fire going. That's why repentance not only always precedes revival but also is always a part of continuing revival. When sin is removed and continues to be removed, the spiritual fire can burn.

On the other hand, where there is sin; God can powerfully touch someone's life, but the impact will be short lived. For example, God can touch someone's life powerfully in a service, but if they go home and are involved in sinful things, the fire will go out. Sin is like a wet blanket thrown on a fire causing it to smolder and to go out.

We must remove any sin in our life, and the good news is God will help us in three ways. First, He will convict us of sin in our life. He will tell us what is wrong. Second, He will forgive us. If we admit our sin to Him and are willing to repent and ask His forgiveness; He will forgive us. Third, He will also help us to overcome the sin if we ask Him to.

So, let's not excuse sin in our life, let's not tolerate sin in our life and let's not make provision for sin in our life; but let's remove it! And let's keep removing sin as the Lord reveals it to us.

I remember when we were pastoring, having people come to me saying, "Pastor there has got to be something wrong with me. The closer I get to God, the more sin I find in my life." I assured them that was quite normal. The illustration I used was, "The closer you get to a shining light, the more dirt you see. When you're far away, you can't see the dirt. The closer we get to God the more sin we will find." As we remove the sin, however; the hotter the spiritual fire can burn.

As we remove the hindrance of sin, we keep the fire going.

The Hindrance of Being Comfortable and Self-Satisfied

Becoming comfortable and self-satisfied with the way we are and the way things are can be a hindrance to keeping the spiritual fire going. The attitude becomes "everything is fine, I don't need more of God, I don't need more of the working of His Spirit." The attitude becomes like that of the Laodiceans in Revelation chapter three, who said,

"...I am rich, have become wealthy and have need of nothing..." (Revelation 3:17 NKJV).

Comfortable self-satisfaction is a hindrance to keeping the spiritual fire going, but God helps remove this hindrance too. God begins to stir things in us and around us. He begins to strip away our comfortable self-satisfaction.

God is like the mother eagle that begins to strip away the soft down from inside the nest so the young eaglets will become willing to leave the comforts of where they are and learn to fly and be all God intended them to be.

God is like the cod fishermen I heard about. They wanted to get their fish to their far-away markets still tasting fresh. They first tried packing them in ice and shipping them across the country, but they were soggy and tasteless when they arrived at their destinations. They then tried shipping them in tanks alive, but they still didn't taste good when they arrived at their destinations. Then they discovered that the natural enemy of the codfish is the catfish. They decided to put a catfish into each tank and then ship the fish across the country. When the codfish arrived at their destinations, they tasted great because all through the journey they swam vigorously in their tanks to stay one step ahead of the catfish. Have you ever noticed God is a master at putting "catfish" in our tanks? It keeps us spiritually fresh.

God is like the camper who will periodically stir the campfire in order to keep the fire burning and to make it burn brighter and hotter. At the campsite, we have to periodically stir the fire to keep it going.

As God disrupts our comfort zone, it energizes us to be hungry for more of God, open to more of God, and desperate for more of God. It keeps the fire going.

The Hindrance of a Religious Attitude

It's been concluded that as bad as sin and carnality are, religiosity is just as bad, if not worse. A religious attitude can stifle or quench the fire.

An example of a religious attitude is putting God in a box, erecting boundaries and barriers for God. Limiting what God can and cannot do. Believing that God can only work in certain ways and God can only do certain things.

Another example of a religious attitude is having forms and motions of worship but not having our hearts and minds engaged. Going through the motions outwardly but not being inwardly engaged.

Just going through the motions soon causes the fire to go out.

With God's help, we need to remove and keep removing the hindrances of sin, comfortable self-satisfaction, and religious attitudes. If we want to keep the fire going, we need to remove and keep removing the hindrances.

HAVE COMBUSTIBLE MATERIAL

To keep the campfire going we also need to have combustible material. We need to keep fueling the fire with combustible material such as dry sticks, branches, and logs.

It's also the same in the spiritual realm. We need to keep fueling the spiritual fire with spiritually combustible material. We are to be that spiritually combustible material, ignitable by the Holy Spirit.

Missionary Amy Carmichael prayed, "Make me thy fuel, flame of God,"[1]

Missionary Jim Elliot reportedly said, "…God deliver me from the…asbestos of other things. Saturate me with the oil of Thy Spirit that I may be a flame. Make me thy fuel, flame of God."

Smith Wigglesworth reportedly said, "…if God has His way, we should be like torches…"

Are we combustible? Someone who is highly flammable? Someone who will stay on fire?

So how do we stay on fire? How do we stay combustible?

Stay on Fire by Reading the Word of God

As we read the Word, the Holy Spirit (through the Word) works on our hearts, minds, and attitudes; keeping us combustible. We remain combustible.

As we look back at the Early Church, they kept the fire of the baptism in the Holy Spirit going by being people who were in the Word of God as it was available to them. They read the Word. They studied the Word. Just because they were baptized in the Holy Spirit didn't mean the spiritual fire would automatically keep burning. They had to be in the Word.

Stay on Fire by Spending Time in Prayer

No one has ever kept the spiritual fire going who did not spend time in prayer. In prayer and as a result of prayer, the Holy Spirit works in our hearts, minds, and attitudes; keeping us combustible.

Once again, as we look at the Early Church, they kept the fire going by being people who prayed. They prayed alone, they prayed together, they prayed in their native language, they prayed in the Spirit. They prayed! Just because they were baptized in the Holy Spirit didn't mean the spiritual fire would automatically keep burning. They had to be people of prayer.

Stay on Fire by Being Surrendered and Open to Jesus

The spiritual fire will not keep burning if we live for ourselves. To remain combustible and keep the spiritual fire burning, we need to continue to die to self and live for Christ. Paul said,

"...I die daily." (I Corinthians 15:31 NKJV).

"...those who live should no longer live for themselves, but for Him who died for them and rose again." (II Corinthians 5:15 NKJV).

Self-centeredness, stubbornness, and rebellion will quench the fire.

The Early Church kept the fire going by being submitted and surrendered to Christ. They wanted God to work in them and through them.

To start a fire and keep it burning there must be combustible material. In the spiritual realm, we are to be that combustible material. We need to be -

- people who read the Word
- people who pray
- people who are surrendered and open to Jesus

HAVE OXYGEN

The third thing you need in order to start a fire and to keep it going is oxygen. When camping, after lighting the fire the first night, when we get up the next morning, the flame is nowhere to be seen. We then have to get a stick and stir the coals. In the coals, we'll find a glowing ember. We'll then get some combustible material like sticks and paper and put them next to the glowing ember.

Then we'll fan that glowing ember with a towel until the glowing ember bursts into a flame that catches the sticks and paper on fire. The fire is burning for another day. The next morning we'll repeat the process and each morning after that.

What are we doing when we fan the glowing ember with a towel? We're putting extra oxygen on the ember and soon it bursts into a flame.

The same principle applies to a charcoal grill. You need to have oxygen to keep the fire going. If you close the vent holes the fire goes out because you've cut off the oxygen supply.

In the spiritual realm, we need spiritual oxygen to keep the fire going. We need the wind of the Holy Spirit.

Jesus said,

"The wind blows where it wishes and you hear the sound of it, but cannot tell where it comes from and where it goes. So is everyone who is born of the Spirit." (John 3:8 NKJV).

When Luke described what happened on the day of Pentecost when the baptism in the Holy Spirit was poured out, he wrote,

"And suddenly there came a sound from heaven, as of a rushing mighty wind, and it filled the whole house where they were sitting." (Acts 2:2 NKJV).

To start a spiritual fire and to keep it going, we need the Holy Spirit. We can't work up the fire on our own. We can't start the fire on our own. We can't keep the fire going on our own. We need the Holy Spirit. We need as much of the Holy Spirit's power and working that we can possibly have.

As we stated earlier, every believer has the Holy Spirit dwelling within them. When a person accepts Christ, the Holy Spirit comes and dwells within them. But in addition to that, there is an additional dimension of the working of the Holy Spirit available to every believer—the baptism in the Holy Spirit. The baptism in the Holy Spirit will increase the fire and all that the fire does in the life of a believer.

In the natural realm, how do you increase the temperature of a fire? What do you do? You increase the amount of oxygen. For example, on a charcoal grill, how do you increase the temperature in the grill? You open the vent holes further.

To increase the spiritual fire, we need to open the spiritual vent holes. We need to increase the spiritual oxygen. Be baptized in the Holy Spirit.

We can't expect to have the fire of the Early Church without the baptism in the Holy Spirit the Early Church had. We need to have what they had in order to be what they were and to do what they did.

If we have been baptized in the Holy Spirit, we need to stay fresh in the Holy Spirit as we've discussed in previous chapters. Today's fire cannot burn on yesterday's oxygen. In the natural realm, a fire can't burn today on yesterday's oxygen. There has to be fresh oxygen today.

In the spiritual realm, we need the fresh winds of the Holy Spirit blowing in our life every day. Pray in the Spirit every day.

When the fresh winds of the Holy Spirit are blowing in our life, the fire will keep burning.

SUMMARY

God is passionate about us.

He comes running to us when we are in need.

"... The Lord is my helper; I will not fear. What can man do to me?" (Hebrews 13:6 NKJV).

The word "helper" has the connotation of "one who comes running". God comes running to you and me in our times of need. Granted there are times we may wish He would have started sooner and gotten there quicker; but He gets there at the right time.

He rejoices over us.

"The Lord your God in your midst the mighty one will save; He will rejoice over you with gladness, He will quiet you with His love, He will rejoice over you with singing." (Zephaniah 3:17 NKJV).

He is jealous for us.

"For the Lord your God is a consuming fire, a jealous God." (Deuteronomy 4:24 NKJV).

The connotation of "jealous over us" is that God is passionate about us.

He thinks about us.

"How precious are Your thoughts to me, Oh God! How great are the sum of them! If I should count them, they would be more in number than the sand... " (Psalm 139:17-18 NKJV).

A person thinks about what they are passionate about. God thinks about us!

God is passionate about us, and He wants us to be passionate about Him! That passion for God will then do what fire does in the natural realm.

- The fire will attract others to what we have

   Wherever you find a fire, it attracts people. A spiritual fire burning in our life attracts others to what we have.

- The fire will strengthen us

   You put steel into a fire to strengthen it. A spiritual fire strengthens us, makes us strong.

- The fire will purify us

   You put ore in a fire to purify it. A spiritual fire has a purifying effect on our life. We want to be right with God.

- The fire will melt us

   You put metal in a fire to soften it. A spiritual fire softens our hearts toward God.

- The fire will influence those around us

   A fire influences the people around it. For example, it warms them. People on fire for Jesus have an influence on those around them.

- The fire gets results

   A fire has an impact. Things happen as a result of fire. Spiritual fire, passion, gets results. It was the passion of the women with the issue of blood that drove her through the crowd to touch the hem of Jesus' garment for her healing. It was the passion of the man who had guests come at midnight that drove him to keep knocking on his neighbor's door until the neighbor got up and gave him the bread he needed. It was the passion of the woman who kept coming before the unjust judge until she received justice. James said,

> "... *The effective, fervent prayer of a righteous man avails much*" (James 5:16 NKJV).

James is saying the passionate prayer of a righteous man gets results.

- The fire will result in power

Passion produces power. Power follows passion. Jentezen Franklin said, "You cannot be passive or stoic about your faith and experience a manifestation of His resurrection power in your life." Passion leads to power.[2]

REVIEW AND DISCUSSION QUESTIONS

1. What are the three requirements for keeping a fire going in the natural?

2. What are some things people are on fire about?

3. What does it mean to be on fire for Jesus?

4. What are some of the hindrances to the spiritual fire in our lives?

5. How do we become and remain spiritually combustible material?

6. What is the spiritual oxygen?

7. How do we increase the temperature of the spiritual fire in our life?

Chapter Eleven

WALKING IN STEP WITH THE SPIRIT

L arry was a truck driver whose lifelong dream was to fly. He joined the Air Force but poor eyesight kept him grounded. One day, sometime later, he got a brainstorm. He went to the local Army/Navy surplus store and bought a tank of helium and forty-five weather balloons. These were heavy-duty balloons measuring more than four feet across when fully inflated. Larry used straps to attach the balloons to his lawn chair. He anchored the chair to the bumper of his jeep and inflated the balloons. He packed some sandwiches, drinks, and a loaded BB gun, figuring he could pop some of the balloons when he wanted to return to earth. His preparations were complete, Larry sat in his chair and cut the anchoring cord, thinking he would float lazily upward. But it didn't work out that way. When he cut the cord, he shot up as if fired from a cannon. Up to eleven thousand feet he soared. At that height, he could not risk deflating any of the balloons. So he stayed up for fourteen hours not knowing how to get down.

He eventually drifted into the approach corridor over L.A. International Airport. A commercial pilot radioed the tower that he saw a guy in a lawn chair at eleven thousand feet holding a gun in his lap. Helicopters finally towed him safely back down, where he was immediately arrested. A reporter called out to him, "Sir, why did you do that?" Larry replied, "Hey, a man can't just sit around."

What a great story, and a great truth! Life is too short to just "sit around". Eternity will last forever. The question is, "What are you doing for eternity's sake?"[1]

God wants to use every believer to touch the lives of those around us for eternity's sake. To enable us to do that to the fullest dimension, He provided the baptism in the Holy Spirit, which gives us the power, the ability, the enablement.

In order for us to be used to the fullest dimension and for the working of the baptism in the Holy Spirit to work through us in the fullest possible way, we must walk in step with the Spirit.

Galatians 5:25 says,

"... let us also walk in the Spirit" (NKJV).

Elisha is an example of someone who walked in the Spirit. We find principles and keys for walking in step with the Spirit as we look at the life of Elisha.

WHAT ELISHA WAS

We find the account of Elisha in II Kings beginning in chapter two. Elisha was an assistant to the prophet Elijah. The Lord was going to take Elijah home to heaven, and somehow Elisha knew that. Elisha followed Elijah to Gilgal, to Bethel, to Jericho and then to the Jordan River.

When they came to the Jordan River, Elijah took off the mantle he was wearing. The mantle was an outer garment made of wool or cotton and was worn over the head or shoulders as a shawl. Elijah rolled up the mantle and struck the water. The river parted, and they walked across on dry ground – an incredible miracle.

When they got to the other side, Elijah said to Elisha, "What can I do for you before I am taken?" Elisha said, "Please let a double portion of your spirit be upon me."

Elijah said, "You have asked a difficult thing, but if you see me when I am taken you will have it. If not, you won't."

Then it happened! As they were walking and talking, suddenly a chariot of fire appeared with horses of fire, separating the two of them, and Elijah went up into heaven in a whirlwind. He was gone. As we look at the life of Elisha, we find three characteristics that are important if we are going to be people who walk in step with the Spirit.

Elisha Was Committed to God

Elisha was first and foremost committed to God. He was going to serve God whether Elijah was there or not. If Elijah was there, great, they would serve God together. If Elijah was gone, he was still going to serve God. No matter what, he was going to serve God!

There are some today who serve God only if their spouse serves God, or only if their friends serve God. If their spouse no longer serves God, they no longer serve

God. If their spouse dies, they no longer serve God. If their friends no longer serve God, they no longer serve God. If their friends move away, they no longer serve God.

We need to get beyond that to where we are committed to serving God. It doesn't matter who joins us, it doesn't matter who drops out, we commit to serving God.

Our mindset needs to follow the words of the old chorus, "I have decided to follow Jesus, no turning back. Though no one join me, still I will follow. The world behind me, the cross before me."[2]

Jonathan Edwards, a well-known hero from church history, said, "I wish everyone would serve God, but if they won't, I still will."

Elisha was committed to God. People walking in step with the Spirit are committed to God.

Elisha Was Desirous of God

When Elisha was asked by Elijah, "What do you want?" Instead of asking for riches, fame or popularity; he asked for more of God. He wanted a double portion of the Spirit of God that was in Elijah. He wanted more of the Spirit.

How would many believers answer that question today? You can have anything you want. Sad to say, many would say; I want more money, I want a better job, I want a bigger house. There is nothing wrong with any of these things but may our greatest desire be, I want more of God. I want more of His Spirit.

Unfortunately today, believers often desire more what God can give them and do for them than desiring God.

People walking in step with the Spirit are desirous of God. Elisha was desirous of God.

Elisha Was Enduring With God

As we look at the account of Elisha we find that he was enduring with God. Undoubtedly, Elisha would have had a myriad of questions. Things he didn't understand. God, why did you take Elijah? God, why am I still here? God, why? God, why?

Have you noticed that we don't follow Jesus very long before we realize there are a lot of questions? There are many mysteries we don't understand. But we need to keep following. We need to keep serving. In spite of the questions. In spite of the mysteries.

I heard veteran missionary, Charles Greenaway, summarize it like this, "It's not worth going to hell over a mystery." Are there questions? Yes. Are there mysteries? Yes. Are there things we don't understand? Yes, all kinds of them. But we keep following. We keep serving. We don't quit. We don't give up.

Several years ago an Olympian from an African nation ran in a distance race in the Olympics here in America. Early in the race he fell and was badly hurt. He got up, however, and continued to run the race, but the longer the race went on the further behind he fell. After some time, the winner crossed the finish line, and the awards were presented to the top finishers. The fans left the stands. Meanwhile, this runner from Africa kept running even though the race was done and the stands were now empty. Finally, he crossed the finish line. Later, he was asked, "Why did you keep on going?" He said, "My country did not send me 5,000 miles to start, they sent me 5,000 miles to finish."

Jesus didn't die on a cross just so you and I would start. He died on a cross so we would finish! In order to finish, we need to be enduring with God. We need to keep going in spite of the questions and mysteries.

Nowhere in the Bible does God promise us that He would always make sense! In fact, He promised us the opposite. He said,

> *"For My thoughts are not your thoughts, Nor are your ways my ways, "says the Lord. For as the heavens are higher than the earth, so are My ways higher than your ways, and My thoughts than your thoughts."* (Isaiah 55:8-9 NKJV).

He didn't promise us He would make sense. But He did promise us that He would be with us and that we would make it through whatever the situation is.

If we are going to walk in step with the Spirit, we need to be enduring with God. Elisha was enduring with God.

WHAT ELISHA DID

As we continue the account of Elisha, we find that Elijah has gone up to heaven and Elisha is left on the bank of the Jordan River. Elisha picks up the mantle of Elijah that had fallen when he was taken up to heaven. Elisha then stands on the bank of the river holding the mantle.

Perhaps he was looking at the river that was flowing again. Or looking at the mantle he held. Or remembering how a few moments earlier Elijah had swung the mantle and God had parted the waters of the river.

Perhaps Elisha was wondering, "Can God work through me?"

We too will stand and ask, "Can God work through me?" "Can God use me?"

Elisha stood at a point of decision. He could keep holding the mantle. He could drop the mantle and walk away. Or, he could swing the mantle and see what God could do.

We read that Elisha swung the mantle and struck the waters of the Jordan River. When he did, the waters parted! Another incredible miracle!

The key was, he stepped out in faith and swung the mantle. He did something he had never done before, and he saw God do through him something he had never seen God do through him before.

Some phrases I have heard over the years come to mind. "If we don't do what we have never done, we will never get what we have never gotten." "If we keep doing what we have always done, we will keep getting what we have always gotten." "To get what we have never had, we have to do what we have never done."

Now, we're not saying "just do something." We need to be led by the Holy Spirit. We need to have a directive, a word from God. But then, as He leads, we need to be willing to step out and act. We need to be willing to "swing the mantle."

I think of Peter on the night Jesus came walking on the water to the disciples who were out in their boat in the middle of the sea. As impulsive as Peter was, he knew he couldn't just jump out of the boat and start walking on the water. Peter called out to Jesus and said, "Invite me to come to you." Jesus said, "Come." Peter stepped out of the boat and walked on the water.

Peter received a word from Jesus and then he stepped out of the boat. Upon receiving the word from Jesus, he did something he had never done before. He got out of the boat while it was still in the middle of the sea, and he saw something he had never seen before. He saw himself walking on the water.

Someone might say, "But he sank." Remember, he didn't sink because he got out of the boat and walked on the water. He sank because he took his eyes off Jesus.

Besides, I think someone said it well when they said, "I would rather be a wet water-walker than a dry boat-sitter any day."

We need to be willing to step out and swing the mantle as the Holy Spirit leads us. It may be to step out and speak to someone God leads you to speak to. It may be to step out and pray for someone God is leading you to pray for. It may be to step out and give to someone or something God has put on your heart. It may be to step out and be used in a gift of the Holy Spirit. It may be to step out and do a certain ministry.

The possibilities are endless, but we will never see what God can do unless we are willing to step out and swing the mantle. Don't let fear stop you! Step out and swing the mantle!

Let me illustrate with a deer hunting illustration. It's deer hunting season, you're in the woods in a legal hunting area and you have a deer hunting license. You have a rifle in your hands. You have bullets in the rifle. And, you have a deer standing right in front of you. But, unless you pull the trigger you will never shoot a deer.

Here's the application. You can be baptized in the Holy Spirit. You can be a person who prays in the Spirit. You can be a person who desires the Holy Spirit to work through you. You can have and do everything we have talked about in this book thus far, but unless you step out and "swing the mantle," unless you follow the leading of the Holy Spirit; you will never see what God could have done.

Now, do things always turn out the way we thought they would when we step out and swing the mantle? Oh my, no! There are plenty of questions, mysteries, and surprises here too. But God knows what He is doing, and our part is that we need to be willing to follow His leading.

We need to be willing to step out and swing the mantle. If we don't, we'll never see what God could have done. Elisha swung the mantle.

WHAT ELISHA SAW

When Elisha stepped out and swung the mantle, what did he see?

Elisha Saw a Miracle

When Elisha stepped out and swung the mantle, he saw a miracle. The waters of the Jordan River parted. It's great to hear of miracles, but it's even greater to be a part of a miracle. As Elisha stepped out and swung the mantle he was part of a miracle, not just a spectator.

As we step out on the leading of the Lord, we too will see God do amazing things. There are miracles waiting to happen when we step out as the Holy Spirit leads.

Elisha Saw Wisdom

We find later that the men of the city came to Elisha and said, the city is good, but the water is bad. The water causes death and barrenness. Elisha said, "Bring me a new bowl and put salt in it." They brought him a new bowl with salt in it, he poured it into the source of the water, and the water was healed. Another incredible miracle.

First, notice the leading of the Lord. The Lord gave him wisdom as to what to do. Then also notice, he had to act upon it. He had to "swing the mantle." He had to ask for the bowl with salt in it and then he had to pour it into the source of the water. The wisdom would have done him no good unless he stepped out and acted upon it.

God can give us the wisdom to do whatever He is asking us to do. Of course, we should plan, prepare, and study the best we can, but above and beyond that; God can give us the wisdom to do what He asks us to do.

Elisha Saw Protection

One day as Elisha was walking down the road, some young men mocked him. They called out to Elisha, "go on up you bald head." Most likely they were referring to how Elijah had earlier gone up in the whirlwind and apparently Elisha was bald.

The Bible says that two female bears came out of the woods and mauled forty-two of the young men. We see here that God was going to protect Elisha's reputation and respect. God took care of those who were mocking and disrespectful.

Elisha saw God's protection, and we too will see God's protection.

SUMMARY

When Elisha was asked by Elijah, "What do you want?" Elisha said he wanted a double portion of the Spirit that was in Elijah. We look at Elisha and say, I want to walk in step with the Spirit like Elisha.

May our prayer and desire be that I want to walk in step with the Spirit in such a way that people would desire what I have. I heard George Wood, General Superintendent of the Assemblies of God, say, "Early Pentecostals never tried to argue people into the baptism in the Holy Spirit, they just lived in such a way that people wanted what they had."

Lord help us to walk in step with the Spirit.

Help us to be like Elisha:

- committed to God
- desirous of God
- enduring with God

Help us to be like Elisha, to be willing to step out and swing the mantle, to step out in obedience as the Lord leads.

Help us to see like Elisha:

- the miraculous of God manifested
- the wisdom of God manifested
- the protection of God manifested

REVIEW AND DISCUSSION QUESTIONS

1. What does God want to do through the life of every believer?

2. Name three character traits of Elisha and discuss each trait.

3. If we are desirous of God, how is it expressed in our life?

4. What does it mean to be "enduring with God"?

5. How do we know if God is asking us to do something (to swing the mantle)?

6. How do we handle it when things turn out differently than we thought when we swing the mantle?

Chapter Twelve

MINISTERING THE BAPTISM IN THE HOLY SPIRIT

I remember hearing an old adage that said, "If you give a man a fish, you have fed him a meal; if you teach a man how to fish you have fed him for life."

In a similar way, if we teach people how to minister the baptism in the Holy Spirit; the ministry is exponentially multiplied.

After serving twenty years as a Lead Pastor and then traveling across America and overseas as an evangelist since 1998, primarily ministering on the baptism in the Holy Spirit, there are some things I have observed and learned over the years.

In this chapter, I want to pass on some of the things I have learned regarding ministering the baptism in the Holy Spirit. Things that can help a person receive if they have not already received themselves and also things that can help a person minister the baptism in the Holy Spirit to others. It would be a shame to experience this wonderful life-changing experience and not want to or know how to pass it on to others.

In this chapter we want to look at:

- the messenger
- the message
- the ministry

THE MESSENGER

In Acts 19:1 we see the messenger was the Apostle Paul

"...that Paul, having passed through the upper regions, came to Ephesus..." (NKJV).

In Ephesus, Paul ministered the baptism in the Holy Spirit to the followers of Christ that he found there.

As we look at the life of Paul in the New Testament, we find five important qualities of a messenger of the baptism in the Holy Spirit.

Be a Believer in Christ

This one is obvious. A person needs to be a believer in Christ. Paul was a believer.

Be a Believer in the Baptism in the Holy Spirit

We need to believe the baptism in the Holy Spirit is real. We need to believe the baptism in the Holy Spirit is important. We need to believe the baptism in the Holy Spirit is for today. Paul modeled this. The early church modeled this. It's very hard, or even impossible, to minister something we don't believe.

Be Baptized in the Holy Spirit

I used to believe this was absolutely required until a few years ago. After reading Charles Parham's testimony, I changed my mind. In December of 1900, Charles Parham was looking for the Biblical evidence of the baptism in the Holy Spirit. Parham found it after a morning of prayer at his Bethel Bible College. A student, Agnes Ozman, asked him to lay hands on her and pray for her to be baptized in the Holy Spirit. Parham said he at first hesitated at her request, "not having the experience myself." Nevertheless, after being further pressed to do so, he laid hands on her and prayed for her, and she began speaking in tongues.[1]

While it may not be absolutely required to have been baptized in the Holy Spirit ourselves, I sincerely believe that it helps to have experienced it ourselves. It's hard to minister something we have not experienced ourselves.

Be a Person of Prayer

Prayer develops a relationship of confidence in God. The greatest benefit of prayer is not what God does but the relationship with God that develops. As our relationship with God develops, our confidence in God grows. We are able to minister with greater confidence.

Paul was a man of prayer. As a result, he had an intimate relationship with God that enabled him to minister with confidence in God.

Be Clean Before God and Man

It's hard to minister in confidence if things are not right between us and God and us and other people. We need to be clean before God. We need to be clean before others.

We also need to have clean motives. Not like Simon, the sorcerer, in Acts 8:9-24.

Paul strove to be clean before God and man. Paul said,

"...I myself always strive to have a conscience without offense toward God and men." (Acts 24:16 NKJV).

THE MESSAGE

Regarding the message, there are some basic principles that apply whether we are ministering to an individual or to a group and whether it's to adults, teens or children.

We often find people:

- who don't know what the baptism in the Holy Spirit is
- who don't know what the baptism in the Holy Spirit can do
- who don't know the baptism in the Holy Spirit is for them
- who don't know how to receive the baptism in the Holy Spirit

Therefore we need to:

- share what the baptism in the Holy Spirit is
- share what the baptism in the Holy Spirit can do
- share that the baptism in the Holy Spirit is for them

- share how to receive the baptism in the Holy Spirit

Also, include your testimony or the testimony of others whose testimony those you are sharing with can relate to. For example, if sharing with children, share testimonies of children who have received the baptism in the Holy Spirit. If sharing with teens, share testimonies of teens who have received the baptism in the Holy Spirit.

In the testimony, include:

- background that relates to those you are sharing with
- how the baptism in the Holy Spirit was received
- what the baptism in the Holy Spirit has done

THE MINISTRY

After sharing about the baptism in the Holy Spirit, we now come to ministering the baptism in the Holy Spirit. We have divided this section into four parts:

- the invitation
- the instructions
- the prayer
- the follow-up

The Invitation

If we want to see people receive the baptism in the Holy Spirit, we need to give them an invitation. Yes, God can sovereignly pour out His Holy Spirit as He did in Acts 10:44-48 when the Holy Spirit fell as Peter was preaching in Cornelius' house and they began speaking in tongues.

Also, people can receive on their own when they are by themselves. Just like I did walking across a field in the middle of the night while attending a secular university. We often hear testimonies of people who have been baptized in the Holy Spirit alone at their bedside, in their car, in the shower, and in various other places.

We will see more people receive the baptism in the Holy Spirit, however, if we give them an opportunity. I remember a time in our first pastorate when I was complaining to the Lord that no one was being baptized in the Holy Spirit. The Lord said, "You're not giving them a chance." After that, I started to give people an opportunity and people started getting baptized in the Holy Spirit.

In the invitation, stress the choice is theirs. No one is forcing them or making them; not God, not the church and not you.

Then let them know what you will do. That you will explain a couple of things to them and then you're going to pray for them.

The Instructions

Just as we give instructions to people who want to give their life to Christ, we give instructions to people who desire to receive the baptism in the Holy Spirit. Of course, people can give their life to Christ without any instructions, but usually, we will tell them what we are going to do and explain to them how to receive Christ.

People can also be baptized in the Holy Spirit without any instructions as they were at Cornelius' house in Acts 10 or as I was walking across a field in the middle of the night at a secular university. On the other hand, instructions can be very helpful in preparing people to receive the baptism in the Holy Spirit. We have found that without instructions, people often just stand there like a deer caught in the headlights not knowing what to do or what to expect and often times even doing things that would hinder their receiving, like clenching their teeth.

Over the years we have found many who sought the baptism for years receive the baptism in our services. Afterward, they have told us that no one ever explained to them how to receive. Once they received some simple instructions and knew what to expect and how to receive the baptism, it happened easily. So what are the instructions?

Once they indicate that they want prayer for the baptism in the Holy Spirit, encourage them with the fact that God wants to baptize them in the Holy Spirit even more than they want to receive it. I heard an old-time Pentecostal preacher say, "There are only two reasons a person who is seeking will not be baptized in the Holy Spirit - (1) lack of faith or (2) lack of being yielded."

There is no example in scripture of anyone who wanted to be baptized in the Holy Spirit, and God said "no." Just as there is no example of someone wanting to get saved and God said "no."

In the instructions, we are trying to remove the barriers because it's not a matter of God wanting to, it's a matter of a person being yielded.

Then we share two practical keys based on Acts 2:4.

"And they were all filled with the Holy Spirit and began to speak with other tongues, as the Spirit gave them utterance" (NKJV).

Two Practical Keys

One – notice the words "they" and "them" in Acts 2:4. In this verse, God didn't speak in tongues. The angels didn't speak in tongues. They, the 120 in the upper room, began to speak in tongues. Here's the principle. People can't speak anything as long as their mouths are shut, their teeth are clenched, and their jaws are locked. We have to open our mouths, move our tongues, and put a voice to it in order to speak our native language or to speak in tongues.

I share with those I am praying for that I was prayed for in church to receive the baptism in the Holy Spirit, and nothing happened. It wasn't God's fault. It was my fault. My mouth was shut, my teeth were clenched, and my jaw was locked, yet I was wondering why nothing was happening. A carpenter couldn't have gotten my mouth open with a crowbar. A few weeks later I was praying out loud for the baptism in the Holy Spirit, and the "baptism" came quickly and easily. They key was, my mouth was open, my tongue was moving, and my voice was engaged.

I then tell the people that we're going to do what they were doing in the upper room, they were praying. Part of praying is praising and worshipping God. We tell them that in a few moments, we're going to ask them to close their eyes to minimize distractions, to lift their hands and to begin to praise and worship the Lord out loud. We share with them how this will get them to open their mouth, to move their tongue and to engage their voice.

Two – we share with them how a person can't speak two languages at the same time. A person can't speak in their native language and speak in tongues at the same time. There can only be one language coming out of a person's mouth at a time. I tell people, "When I come to the end of praying for them, stop worshipping in your native language. Stop your native language because you can't speak two languages at the same time."

The Prayer

We then tell them that after we have briefly praised and worshiped the Lord out loud in our native language, then I'm going to pray a short simple prayer asking the Lord to baptize them in the Holy Spirit. When I come to the end of the prayer, I'm going to begin to pray in tongues. When I begin to pray in tongues, at that time, stop worshipping in your native language. Open your mouth, move your tongue, and put a voice to the words that are there in another language. I encourage people

- don't try to figure out what to say
- don't worry what it sounds like
- don't try to think of what you're going to say next
- just boldly step out in faith and speak the language the Lord gives you
- it will sound strange to you
- you will not know what you are saying

Those words in another language are the first physical evidence that they have been baptized in the Holy Spirit.

There are two reasons I pray in tongues after praying for them in their native language. First, I am praying for them for things I may not be aware of; such as fear, hindrances, etc. Second, it sets them at ease to begin to speak in other tongues.

If they haven't stopped worshipping in their native language when asked to do so, I will then often ask them to just take a deep breath to get them to stop and then ask them to begin to speak the language the Lord is giving them.

As they begin to speak in other tongues, I then encourage them to keep going for awhile.

The Follow-Up

After they have prayed in tongues for a while, I then share some follow-up instructions with them. Just as we give new converts to Christ follow-up instructions to prevent the enemy from stealing from them or confusing them regarding what they have just received, we do the same for those who have just been baptized in the Holy Spirit for the same reason. So the enemy does not steal from them or confuse them regarding what they have received. I share four things with them.

- *Don't let anyone talk you out of what you have just received.* Not the devil. Not other people. Not yourself. If you were speaking in an unknown language, you were baptized in the Holy Spirit.
- *Don't base the reality of what you experienced on what you did or did not feel.* The initial physical evidence of the baptism in the Holy Spirit is not what a person feels but that they spoke in other

tongues. Some people, when they are baptized in the Holy Spirit, in addition to speaking in other tongues, feel warm. Others feel like they've been hit with a jolt of electricity. My reaction was completely the opposite. I said, "Oh that was nice." That was it! But it was just as real!

- *Put to use every day what you have received.* Whether it's a word, a phrase, a sentence or a full language; put to use every day what you have received. Every day take time to pray in tongues. Don't get hung up on how few or how many words you may have but just put to use what you have. As you put it to use, the language will grow. Words become phrases. Phrases become sentences. Sentences become a language. Also, two things that will help the language grow are (1) pray out loud and (2) slow down. As you pray out loud and slow down, you will find new words forming.

- *If you have any questions, don't hesitate to ask.* Ask someone you know who is a well-respected, mature spirit-filled believer if you have any questions.

Also, if there are those you prayed with who did not receive the baptism in the Holy Spirit, encourage them (1) that God loves them, (2) that God wants to baptize them in the Holy Spirit and (3) that God will baptize them in the Holy Spirit if they stay open and keep seeking. It may happen at church, in their car, at their bedside, or even in the shower.

SUMMARY

The baptism in the Holy Spirit is essential for a believer to be all God intended them to be and the baptism in the Holy Spirit is for believers of all ages; adults, teens, and children.

God wants to use us to share with others what we have received and to pray with them so they too can receive. If we don't step out and minister the baptism in the Holy Spirit; individuals miss out and suffer, the church misses out and suffers, and the kingdom of God misses out and suffers.

Wherever and whenever God opens the doors and prompts us, let's minister the baptism in the Holy Spirit.

REVIEW AND DISCUSSION QUESTIONS

1. What are the five qualities that the messenger should have? Discuss each one.

2. What should be included in the message on the "baptism" as we share with people?

3. What should a typical testimony include?

4. What are two practical instructions based on Acts 2:4?

5. After the practical instructions, what do you do? What are the steps?

6. What are the four follow-up points?

7. What do you tell those who did not receive?

Chapter Thirteen

GOING WITH THE GREATEST

In his book *Share Jesus Without Fear*, William Fay tells of how one day he had a layover at an airport, so he went to the Red Carpet room to wait for his flight to be called. There he saw Mohammed Ali sitting at a table with a briefcase full of tracts about Islam. Fay said he stopped to visit with Ali. Ali gave him a couple of his pamphlets and signed his name. Because of his illness, Parkinson's disease, it took him a long time to sign the pamphlets.

Fay said that as he watched Ali signing the pamphlets, he thought, "Here is a man giving his all with what little physical and mental abilities he has left, to share a lie..."[1]

The Muslims have a slogan, "evangelizing the world, doing whatever it takes." And that, to share a lie.

Followers of Jesus have the truth, and we have been given the power of the Holy Spirit to share the truth. Our slogan ought to be, "evangelizing the world, doing whatever it takes."

According to Fay, however, in an average church as few as 5% to 10% of the people have shared their faith in the past year.[2]

On the other hand, according to an article I read, in Pentecostal and Charismatic churches, 80% have shared their faith with someone in the past year. What accounts for the difference? I submit to you that the difference is the baptism in the Holy Spirit.

Jesus said, regarding the baptism in the Holy Spirit,

"...you will receive power when the Holy Spirit comes on you; and you will be my witnesses..." (Acts 1:8 NIV).

The baptism in the Holy Spirit gives us the power to be the witnesses Jesus wants us to be. We have the greatest power, to share the greatest message, using the greatest method, and have the greatest motivation.

THE GREATEST MESSAGE

In Luke 4:16-22, Jesus came to the city of Nazareth, the city where He had been brought up, and as His custom was, He went to the synagogue on the Sabbath Day. He stood up and read from the Book of Isaiah a portion of scripture that referred to Him, Isaiah 61:1-3.

Jesus read,

"The Spirit of the Lord is upon Me, because He has anointed Me to preach the gospel to the poor; He has sent Me to heal the brokenhearted, to proclaim liberty to the captives and recovery of sight to the blind, to set at liberty those who are oppressed; to

proclaim the acceptable year of the Lord." (Luke 4:18-19 NKJV).

The Holy Spirit had anointed Him. The general word translated as "anointed" means "any kind of rub down." In a general sense, it would be like someone covering himself with oil or lotion. Here, however, it would refer to being covered with the Holy Spirit. The Holy Spirit had anointed Jesus, and the Holy Spirit desires to anoint us. For what?

The next phrase says "to preach." Jesus was anointed to preach. To preach simply means to proclaim. Jesus was anointed to preach, and the Holy Spirit desires to anoint all believers to preach. Not all believers will preach at a pulpit in a church; but we are all called to be preachers, proclaimers. Of what?

The next phrase says "the gospel." The gospel simply means "good news." All believers are called to preach, to proclaim the gospel. The message of the Bible is good news for anyone who accepts it. Without the gospel, people are in bad news and are headed for worse news. Jesus was anointed to preach the gospel and so are we. To whom?

The next phrase says "to the poor." That's one of the beauties of the gospel. It's available to anyone. Rich or poor, any race, any nationality, to anyone. The poor are often excluded from many things. They can't afford them. Not so with the gospel. In fact, the poor are often the most open of anyone. Jesus was anointed by the Holy Spirit to preach the gospel to the poor and so are we.

Most translations then put a semi-colon after the word "poor" as if to imply that the following statements are an explanation of what has just been stated. As we look at it in that way, we see four phrases that illustrate and explain what the good news is. Things we find Jesus did in His earthly ministry, things Jesus does in our life, and things Jesus can do in the life of those we share the gospel with.

Healing to the Brokenhearted

The word translated "brokenhearted" meant "to rub" or to "cause to splinter or crush." There are a lot of things in life that can rub on a person's heart. To rub to the point of hurting, like new shoes can rub on a person's foot to the point of hurting. There are other things that can make a person's heart feel crushed. The good news is Jesus came to heal the broken-hearted. He did it in His earthly ministry and He still heals the broken-hearted today. Our message to the hurting is, Jesus can heal the broken heart.

Liberty to the Captives

Many things can hold a person captive. Some are captives to addictions; such as drugs, alcohol, pornography, etc. Others are captives to unforgiveness or bitterness. Some are captives to hurts from the past; rape, abuse, incest, etc. Others are captives to sin. The good news is Jesus came to set the captive free. He came to deliver the captive and set them free. Our message to the captive is, Jesus can set you free.

Recovery of Sight to the Blind

People can be blind in a couple of ways. People can be spiritually blind. Spiritually not see their sin, their spiritual condition and their need of Jesus. Not realizing that they are lost, that they are separated from God. Not realizing that without Jesus they have no relationship with God in this life, and they have no chance of getting to heaven when this life ends. Jesus, however, can open spiritually blind eyes; enabling people to see their sin, to see their condition, to see their need of Him in order to have a relationship with God in this life and to have a home waiting for them in heaven when this life ends.

People can also be blind physically. Jesus can still open blind eyes. He did it in His earthly ministry, and He can do it today.

Our message to the blind is, Jesus can give you sight.

Liberty to the Oppressed

The word translated as "oppressed" means "shattered." There are many shattered people. Some are shattered because of what someone did to them or said to them. Others are shattered because of what someone did not say or did not do. They were let down. Still others are shattered because of devastating circumstances that have happened. For whatever reason, their lives are shattered.

The good news is, Jesus came to set us free. We can rise above these things. We don't deny the reality of these things. Bad things happen, but we can victoriously rise above them. No longer prisoners. No longer slaves.

In Romans 8:35, Paul lists things that can shatter someone's life,

"... tribulation, or distress, or persecution, or famine, or nakedness, or peril, or sword?" (NKJV).

But then in Romans 8:37 Paul gives us the good news for believers,

"Yet in all these things we are more than conquerors through Him who loved us." (NKJV).

Our message to those whose lives are shattered is, Jesus can set you free. Jesus can help you rise above the circumstances.

The good news of the gospel is Jesus came to bring

- healing for the brokenhearted
- freedom for the captives
- sight for the blind
- deliverance for the shattered

Jesus then concluded by saying He came to proclaim the acceptable year of the Lord. Simply meaning that this was all fulfilled and possible through Him and still is today.

I heard a story years ago about a person who painted on a wall the words, "Jesus is the answer." A few days later someone painted underneath it, "What is the question?" Shortly thereafter another message appeared, "It doesn't matter what the question is, Jesus is the answer."

When our sons were small, Beth would often ask them on the way home from church, "What was the Sunday School lesson about?" They soon learned to simply answer "Jesus." They couldn't go wrong with that answer.

In life, it doesn't matter what the question is, Jesus is the answer!

We have the greatest power, the baptism in the Holy Spirit, to share the greatest message, Jesus.

THE GREATEST METHOD

What is the greatest method of getting out this greatest message?

Surveys tell us that 2% of the people who come to Christ come through non-personal evangelism. Through a television or radio program, through literature or advertising. Thank God for that 2%.

Surveys reveal that 6% of those who come to Christ come through a pastor's influence. Thank God for all the great pastors and for the 6% who come to Christ through their influence.

Surveys also tell us that 6% come to Christ through an outreach program or crusade. Perhaps through a Kids Crusade, Vacation Bible School, or an evangelist, or an evangelistic outreach. Thank God for that 6%.

If you add all these together, you get 14%. So how do the remaining 86% come to Christ?

Surveys reveal that 86% of the people who come to Christ come through a relative, neighbor or friend.[3] In fact in my years of ministering as a pastor and evangelist, I have found that most of those who come to Christ through a pastor or evangelist are in that service because of a friend, neighbor or relative.

God's most effective tool of evangelism is the person who has given his life to Christ and is willing to love and lead others into a relationship with Christ. Believers are more effective than any other method.

I was told about a church that sent their staff to a conference on evangelism. They spent thousands of dollars to learn three great keys for evangelism. The three great keys were:

- love people
- tell them about Jesus
- watch them get saved

We find a beautiful example of this in the life of Philip. In Acts 8 Philip, a layman, one of the original deacons of the Early Church, went to minister in the city of Samaria. There he preached about Jesus to them, and many believed and accepted Christ. Then an angel of the Lord spoke to Philip and sent him to the road between Jerusalem and Gaza. He went from an incredible move of God in Samaria to a road in the desert. From ministering to many to ministering to one individual.

FIVE KEY REASONS WHY PHILIP WAS ABLE TO BE SO USED BY GOD

Philip Was Open

Philip was one of the seven deacons of the Early Church, a man of good reputation, full of the Holy Spirit and wisdom.

"...seven men of good reputation, full of the Holy Spirit and wisdom..." (Acts 6:3 NKJV).

The term deacon literally means "table waiter." It implies serving. The deacons were selected to help with the food distribution of the Early Church so the apostles could devote themselves to prayer and minister the word.

Philip wasn't focused on being a "star" but rather on "serving." He just wanted to serve. It didn't matter if he was ministering to multitudes or to one individual. It didn't matter if it was in the city or on the road in a desert. He just wanted to serve wherever he could or wherever he was needed.

One pastor was asked, "How many deacons does your church have?" He replied, "Our church is filled with deacons, but three of them hold the office." God could use Philip because he was available. He just wanted to serve. He didn't have to be a star.

How open are we to being used by God? How available are we for God to use?

That doesn't mean Philip was a lazy man, doing nothing, just sitting around, with nothing to do. He was as busy as anyone, but he was available for God to use. He was open for God to use. Are we open for God to use us?

Philip Was Willing

When the angel said to Philip "go," he arose and went.

"So he arose and went...." (Acts 8:27 NKJV).

God wants to use us to minister to others more than we realize. We need to be willing to follow through on the appointments the Father sets up. This was a key to Jesus' ministry.

So much of Jesus' ministry seemed to be unplanned and unscheduled but was the result of His being aware of the sovereignty of appointments the Father had arranged. There was the time Jesus met a woman at a well. The time Jesus saw Zacchaeus in a tree. The time Jesus saw Matthew collecting taxes. Jesus saw them as divine appointments the Father had set up, and He was willing to seize the opportunities.

God wants to use us in the same way, but we must be willing. We must be obedient to the voice of the Holy Spirit, obedient to the promptings and nudges of the Holy Spirit.

Philip was willing. Are we willing?

Philip Met People Where They Were

When the Holy Spirit sent Philip to the Ethiopian in the chariot, Philip asked him, "Do you understand what you are reading?" Philip met the Ethiopian where he was in his spiritual life.

I remember a question a man asked me in our first pastorate. He was not a follower of Christ and as I was telling him about Christ, he asked me, "Will you still love me if I don't accept Christ?" I said, "Yes." He didn't give his life to Christ that day, he wasn't ready. But a few months later he did.

Surveys tell us that, on average, a person has to hear the gospel 7.6 times before accepting Christ.[4] I love it when a person is ready and gives his life to Christ when I tell him about Jesus or he gives his life to Christ at an altar call in a service. Many times, however, he may not be ready then. We need to be patient.

A story I read in the God's Word for Today devotional book about Charles and his neighbor Jim illustrates this.

> Charles wanted to tell more people about Jesus, but witnessing scared him. Talking to church members was easy, but speaking to Jim, his neighbor, was a different matter. Jim cared little about God. Charles knew he should share his faith. The burden Charles felt only grew stronger. He even practiced speaking to Jim in the mirror, but everything seemed phony and scripted. He finally decided to just give up, but God had other plans. Later that afternoon, Charles found Jim in his front yard, cussing as he struggled to put up a fence. Charles disregarded his rehearsed presentation and said, "Jim, let me see your shovel for a minute."
>
> Charles helped Jim every day after work. It took two weeks to finish the fence. Each day God gave Charles a few more words to share. Two months later, Jim came to church for the first time. In time, Jim gave his life to Christ. Two years later, Jim became a deacon.[5]

Charles met Jim where he was in his spiritual life. At first, Jim cared little about God. But Charles built a relationship with him and in time was able to share Christ with him.

Philip met the Ethiopian where he was in his spiritual life. In this case the Ethiopian was open and hungry, but he didn't understand what he was reading. Philip was able to immediately explain the scripture to him.

We need to meet people where they are in their spiritual life and start with them there.

Philip Kept the Focus on Jesus

When Philip spoke, his focus was on Jesus, not on secondary issues.

"Then Philip went down to the city of Samaria and preached Christ to them." (Acts 8:5 NKJV).

"Then Philip opened his mouth, and beginning at this Scripture, preached Jesus to him." (Acts 8:35 NKJV).

The most relevant message in the world is "Jesus." We need to keep the focus on Him!

I remember a day in our first pastorate when I was in my office at the church, and there was a knock on the door. I said, "Come in." The door opened, and there was Randy (*name changed*). He was not a part of our church, but I knew who he was. He was one of the biggest smart-aleck's in the area. He was not interested in God and had a smart-aleck comeback for anything a person said. I wondered why he came.

The first words out of his mouth were, "My wife has just left me. Can you give me one good reason why I should not go behind the barn a blow my head off?" I said, "Have a seat and let's talk."

As we were talking, I told Randy, "I'm not going to lie to you and tell you, that if you give your life to Jesus, I can guarantee your wife is going to come back. We have no guarantee of that, but I can tell you that the greatest thing you can do with your life is to make a commitment of your life to Jesus. He has a plan for your life whether your wife comes back or not and when your life on earth is done, He will have a home waiting for you in heaven."

That morning, Randy, the biggest smart-aleck I knew, with tears coming down his cheeks, gave his life to Christ.

We need to keep the focus on Jesus. We can get into arguments and debates about politics and many other things and miss the opportunity before us.

Philip kept the focus on Jesus.

Philip Realized the Ultimate Goal Is Discipleship

Before the Lord moved Philip on to his next assignment, he was there to help begin discipling the Ethiopian.

After hearing of Jesus, the Ethiopian gave his life to Christ. As they traveled along in the Ethiopian's chariot, they came to some water. The Ethiopian wanted to get baptized. Philip said, "If you believe with all your heart, you can be." The Ethiopian said he believed, and he stopped the chariot. They got out, and Philip baptized the Ethiopian.

The goal of evangelism is more than just having someone repeat a prayer to give their life to Christ. It starts there, but the ultimate goal is discipleship.

Jesus said,

"Go therefore and make disciples of all the nations, baptizing them in the name of the Father, and of the Son and of the Holy Spirit, teaching them to observe all things that I have commanded you..." (Matthew 28:19-20 NKJV).

The ultimate goal of evangelism is discipleship.

The greatest method of evangelism is the person who has given his life to Christ, sharing Christ with those around him.

For us to effectively do that, we need to be like Philip. We need to

- be open
- be willing
- meet people where they are at
- keep the focus on Jesus
- realize the ultimate goal of evangelism is discipleship

THE GREATEST MOTIVATION

The greatest motivation is Jesus working in our lives. That's how it was in the Early Church. Jesus changed and impacted their lives, and they shared what Jesus had done with those around them. In the Book of Acts, we read this about the early believers.

"For we cannot but speak the things we have seen or heard" (Acts 4:20 NKJV).

"You have filled Jerusalem with your doctrine" (Acts 5:28 NKJV).

"Those who were scattered went everywhere preaching the Word" (Acts 5:28 NKJV).

We read in the gospels how Jesus touched the lives of individuals early in His ministry before it was time for Him to be publicly revealed. He told them, don't tell anyone. What did they do? They went out and told everyone. Jesus had touched their lives. Jesus had changed their lives. They couldn't keep quiet!

The best thing that can happen to motivate us to share Jesus with those around us is for Jesus to touch our lives with a fresh touch of His Holy Spirit. As we are revived, refreshed and renewed, we impart the message of Jesus to those around us. It's not a chore or duty as much as an overflow of what He has done and is doing in our lives. When we are revived, refreshed and renewed; we go out with the message of Christ.

And the good news is, Jesus goes with us. In Mark 16:20 we read,

"And they went forth and preached everywhere, the Lord working with them and confirming the word with signs following..." (KJV)

Notice the order! As they went, the Lord went with them confirming the word with signs following.

Often we wait for the Lord to do signs, wonders, and miracles—and we wholeheartedly believe He does. But I wonder if the Lord is often waiting for us to go so He can do the signs, wonders, and miracles. Notice again the order. "As they went," came first. The Lord then went with them and confirmed His word with signs followed.

The baptism in the Holy Spirit gives us the power to go and be witnesses for Jesus.

SUMMARY

In Ephesians 4:11 we find a listing of ministry gifts given to the church.

"And He Himself gave some to be apostles, some prophets, evangelists, and some pastors and teachers," (NKJV).

In Ephesians 4:12 we find the purpose.

"for the equipping of the saints for the work of the ministry..." (NKJV).

The goal of church leadership is to equip believers for the work of the ministry. While ministry entails many things, the underlying goal of all ministry is to see people come to Christ.

The good news is that as we share our faith we cannot fail. Bill Fay says in his book *Share Jesus Without Fear* that, "...when you share your faith, you can't fail."[6]

No matter how poorly you think you may have done, know that God can use you and what you said. The devil will tell you, "you should have said this," and "you shouldn't have said that." But God can use the poorest, feeblest presentation that comes from the heart.

Listen to the Apostle Paul's description of his presentation of Christ in Corinth.

"I was with you in weakness, in fear and in much trembling" (I Corinthians 2:3 NKJV).

Sounds like some of us as we present Christ to those around us. But God mightily used what Paul shared with the Corinthians. Even though it was presented in weakness, fear, and trembling. Paul made a difference because He shared the gospel.

Let's do the same. Let's allow the Holy Spirit to work through us. Seeing Him do things through us that we never thought would have been possible. Things that will amaze and astound us.

We have the greatest message—Jesus! And we have been given the greatest power to share that message—the power of the baptism in the Holy Spirit!

Jesus said,

"But you shall receive power when the Holy Spirit has come upon you; and you shall be witnesses to Me in Jerusalem, and in all Judea and Samaria, and to the end of the earth." (Acts 1:8 NKJV).

REVIEW AND DISCUSSION QUESTIONS

1. What do the words "anointed," "preach," and "gospel" mean?

2. What were the four things Jesus said He came to do? How do they apply to today?

3. How do most people come to Christ today?

4. What were the five keys to Philip being used by God?

5. What is the greatest motivation for evangelism?

ENDNOTES

CHAPTER ONE

1. Dan Betzer, "Are You on the Right Plane?" Byline Online (accessed July 31, 2000) www.byline.org.
2. Mary Ann Bird, "Acceptance" (Carol Stream, IL: Leadership, 1995), page 39.
3. Donald Stamps, *Life in the Spirit Study Bible* (Grand Rapids, MI: Zondervan, 2003), page 1618.
4. Craig Brian Larson, *Illustrations for Preaching and Teaching: From Leadership Journal* (Grand Rapids, MI: Baker Books, 1993), page 253.
5. Stamps, *Life in the Spirit Study Bible*, page 1542.
6. George O.Wood, "The Ten T's in an Apostolic Church Plant from Acts 19", *Enrichment Journal* (Springfield, MO: Gospel Publishing House, 2009), pages 25-26.
7. Ibid.
8. Stamps, *Life in the Spirit Study Bible*, pages 1708-1709.

CHAPTER TWO

1. Stamps, *Life in the Spirit Study Bible*, page 1684.
2. Ibid., page 1689.
3. Ibid., page 1692.
4. Ibid.

5. Ibid.

6. Wood, "The Ten T's in an Apostolic Church Plant from Acts 19", pages 25-26.

7. George O. Wood, "A Waterline of Another Kind—Six Marks of a Pentecostal Church," *Enrichment Journal* (Springfield, MO: Gospel Publishing House, 5/6/2011).

8. John McGarvey, "Holy Spirit" (Carol Stream, IL: Leadership, 1995), page 49

CHAPTER FIVE

1. Doyle G. Jones, *Be Filled with the Spirit* (Waxahachie, TX, 1997), pages 31-32.

CHAPTER SIX

1. Michael Brown, *Whatever Happened to the Power of God?* (Shippensburg, PA: Destiny Image, 1991), page 99.

CHAPTER SEVEN

1. David McCasland, "Spray on Mud," *Our Daily Bread* (Grand Rapids, MI: RBC Ministries, February 26).

2. "Pew Forum on Religion and Public Life," *Today's Pentecostal Evangel* (Springfield, MO: Gospel Publishing House, February 18, 2007), page 9.

3. Michael Brown, *Whatever Happened to the Power of God?* (Shippensburg, PA: Destiny Image, 1991), page 99.

4. Ibid.

5. Mahesh Chavda, *The Hidden Power of Speaking in Tongues* (Shippensburg, PA: Destiny Image, 2003), pages 75-76.

6. Adrian Brookes, "One Woman vs The Dragon," *Charisma* (Lake Mary, FL: Charisma Media, March 2008), page 36.

7. Ibid.

8. Ron Auch, "Acts of the Holy Spirit" message, pastor of Prayer House Assembly of God in Kenosha, WI.

9. Brookes, "One Woman vs The Dragon," page 36.

10. Ibid.

11. Carey Benedict, "A Neuroscientific Look at Speaking in Tongues," *New York Times* (November 7, 2006). http://www.nytimes.com/2006/11/07/health/07brain.html?_r=I&scp=2&sq=benedict+carey&st=nyt (accessed January 19, 2011)

12. Wade I. Goodall, *The Blessing* (Lake Mary, FL: Creation House, 2005), pages 50-52.

13. Benedict, "A Neuroscientific Look at Speaking in Tongues," *New York Times* (November 7, 2006).

14. Roberts Liardon, *Why the Devil Doesn't Want You to Pray in Tongues* (Laguna Hills, CA: Embassy Publishing Co, 1999), page 43.

15. George O. Wood, "From the General Secretary" (Springfield, MO: General Secretary's Office, 2003), page 3.

CHAPTER EIGHT

1. "Reaching Muslims in Your Community," News and Resources, *Enrichment Journal* (Springfield, MO: Gospel Publishing House, Summer 2014), page 126.

2. John Welsh, "How Many Christians?" (accessed 12/20/14, www.answers.com).

3. "Islam: Truth or Myth?" (accessed 10/22/15, www.Bible.com).

4. Kimberly Gray, "Around the World there are more Christians" (accessed 10/22/15, www.reporternews.com).

5. Ibid.

6. Del Tarr, "A Linguist Looks at the Mystery of Tongues," *Helping Others Receive the Gift* (Springfield, MO: Access Group, 2008), page 149.

7. Vinson Synan, (accessed 12/20/14, www.ctlibrary.com).

8. *Today's Pentecostal Evangel* (Springfield, MO: Gospel Publishing House, 2006), page 6.

9. Lazarus Chakwera, "Reaching All of Malawi," *Today's Pentecostal Evangel* (Springfield, MO: Gospel Publishing House, 2003), page 4.

10. Wayde I. Goodall, *The Blessing* (Lake Mary, FL: Creation House, 2005), page 10.

CHAPTER NINE

1. Vinson Synan, *The Twentieth-Century Pentecostal Explosion* (Altamonte Springs, FL: Creation House, 1987), page 86.

2. Ibid., page 139.

3. Del Tarr, "A Linguist Looks at the Mystery of Tongues," Helping Others Receive the Gift (Springfield, MO: Access Group, 2008), page 149.

4. Vinson Synan, (accessed 12/20/14, www.ctlibrary.com).

5. Ibid.

6. "All the Gospel into All the World" *PE News* (Springfield, MO: General Council of the Assemblies of God, June 3, 2016).

CHAPTER TEN

1. Amy Charmichael, (accessed 12/20/14, www.goodreads.com).

2. Jentezen Franklin, "The Fasting Edge" *Charisma* (Lake Mary, FL: Media, 2011), pages 69-70.

CHAPTER ELEVEN

1. Dan Betzer, "Larry's Makeshift Airship" Byline Online (accessed 12/10/01, www.byline.org).

2. S. Sundar Singh, chorus "I Have Decided to Follow Jesus," public domain.

CHAPTER TWELVE

1. Mike Clarensau, "News Digest," *Today's Pentecostal Evangel* (Springfield, MO: Gospel Publishing House, 2001), pages 23-24.

CHAPTER THIRTEEN

1. William Fay, *Share Jesus Without Fear* (Nashville, TN: Broadman and Holman Publishers, 1999), page 15.
2. Ibid., page 6.
3. Jeff Brawner, "The Most Effective Tool of Evangelism" MediaLink (Springfield, MO: Gospel Publishing House, 1997), page 4.
4. Mark O. Wilson, *Purple Fish* (Indianapolis, IN: Wesleyan Publishing, 2014), page 134.
5. *God's Word For Today* (Springfield, MO: Gospel Publishing House), page 58.
6. Fay, *Share Jesus Without Fear*, page 12.

ABOUT THE AUTHOR

Bill was born and raised in the Upper Peninsula of Michigan and made a commitment of his life to Christ at the age of ten. He graduated from Northern Michigan University in Marquette, MI with a bachelor's degree in marketing and worked in retail management for three years. While working in the business world Bill met Beth. They were married and have served the Lord together ever since.

After three years in retail management, Bill left the business world to fulfill God's call to the ministry by going to North Central University in Minneapolis, MN. Upon graduation with a bachelor's degree in pastoral studies, Bill accepted a pastorate in Minnesota as Lead Pastor at their first church. During their time there the church grew and entered a building program to triple the size of the sanctuary as people were coming to Christ and being baptized in the Holy Spirit. After eight years as Lead Pastor, Bill resigned to accept the call to his second pastorate.

The second pastorate was located in Wisconsin and Bill served as Lead Pastor there for twelve years. During that time they again saw people come to Christ and baptized in the Holy Spirit as the church reached out with multiple outreaches. During that time Bill and Beth also began to go out ministering on missions trips in America and overseas, bringing church groups with them.

In 1998 God changed the direction of their ministry and called them to travel as evangelists. Since then they have traveled across America and overseas ministering on the baptism in the Holy Spirit and how to live a Spirit-filled life.

You can find more information about Bill and Beth and their ministry by going to their website at:

billjuonifreshfire.com

Sweet Potato Pie

Cook Sweet Potatoes 15-20 min in microwave
slice down center & cool then scoop & put in food processor

1 cup light brown sugar

½ t. salt

4 T unsalted
½ t cinnamon ⎱ Heat in microwave
½ t nutmeg ⎰

1 cup sour cream

3 whole eggs + 2 yolks

1 t van

2 t bourbon

Blend 20 seconds

Pour into pie shell with ¼ c brown sugar sprinkled over bottom of crust as a praline

350° oven

outside set around edges
center jiggles a little bit
Cool 2 hours before slicing

1-800-965-7776
Cooks Country Recipe Book
$19.95